THE PRESIDENTS

VISUAL ENCYCLOPEDIA

Second Edition
DK London

Senior Editor Georgina Palffy **Senior Art Editor** Lynne Moulding
US Editor Megan Douglass **US Executive Editor** Lori Cates Hand
Managing Editor Francesca Baines **Managing Art Editor** Philip Letsu
Senior Production Editor Andy Hilliard **Production Controller** Samantha Cross
Jacket Designer Surabhi Wadhwa **Jacket Design Development Manager** Sophia MTT
Publisher Andrew Macintyre **Art Director** Karen Self
Associate Publishing Director Liz Wheeler **Publishing Director** Jonathan Metcalf

DK Delhi
Editor Shambhavi Thatte **DTP Designer** Pawan Kumar
Senior Editor Virien Chopra **Senior Art Editor** Vikas Chauhan
Managing Editor Kingshuk Ghoshal **Managing Art Editor** Govind Mittal

First Edition
DK Delhi

Project Editor Suefa Lee **Project Art Editor** Divya PR
Assistant Editor Riji Raju **Art Editor** Anjali Sachar
Assistant Art Editors Yashashvi Choudhary, Simar Dhamija
DTP Designers Sachin Gupta, Ashok Kumar
Senior DTP Designer Harish Aggarwal **Picture Researcher** Sakshi Saluja
Jacket Designer Surabhi Wadhwa **Managing Jackets Editor** Saloni Singh
Senior Managing Editor Rohan Sinha **Deputy Managing Art Editor** Anjana Nair

DK London
Assistant Editor Vicky Richards
Senior Editor Fleur Star **Senior Art Editor** Spencer Holbrook
US Senior Editor Margaret Parrish **US Editor** Jill Hamilton
Jacket Editor Claire Gell **Jacket Design Development Manager** Sophia MTT
Producer, Pre-production Nadine King **Producer** Gary Batchelor
Managing Editor Francesca Baines **Managing Art Editor** Philip Letsu
Publisher Andrew Macintyre **Associate Publishing Director** Liz Wheeler
Art Director Karen Self **Publishing Director** Jonathan Metcalf

Written by Philip Parker, Shannon Reed
Consultants: Gary Werner, Philip Baselice
US Sensitivity Reader: Bianca Hezekiah

This American Edition, 2021
First American Edition, 2017
Published in the United States by DK Publishing
1745 Broadway, 20th Floor, New York, NY 10019

Copyright © 2017, 2021 Dorling Kindersley Limited
DK, a Division of Penguin Random House LLC
23 24 25 10 9 8 7 6 5
005–323373–Jan/2021

A catalog record for this book is available from the Library of Congress.
ISBN 978-0-7440-3710-4

DK books are available at special discounts when purchased in bulk
for sales promotions, premiums, fund-raising, or educational use.
For details, contact: DK Publishing Special Markets,
1745 Broadway, 20th Floor, New York, NY 10019
SpecialSales@dk.com

Printed and bound in China

For the curious
www.dk.com

Smithsonian

Established in 1846, the Smithsonian is
the world's largest museum and research
complex, dedicated to public education,
national service, and scholarship in the arts,
sciences, and history. It includes 19 museums
and galleries and the National Zoological
Park. The total number of artifacts, works
of art, and specimens in the Smithsonian's
collection is estimated at 155.5 million.

MIX
Paper | Supporting
responsible forestry
FSC™ C018179

This book was made with Forest
Stewardship Council™ certified
paper – one small step in DK's
commitment to a sustainable future.
For more information go to
www.dk.com/our-green-pledge

THE PRESIDENTS

VISUAL ENCYCLOPEDIA

CONTENTS

1

2

NOTABLE FIRST LADIES 124

3

4

THE CONSTITUTION AND THE PRESIDENCY 146

PRESIDENTIAL PLACES AND VEHICLES 172

5

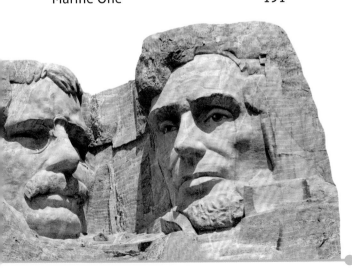

COLOR KEY

This book uses different colors to show the political party of each president.

★ Republican

★ Democrat

★ Other parties or independents

1 PRESIDENTS

Since George Washington took the oath as the first president of the United States in 1789, the country has had 46 presidents. As the nation's chief executive, presidents throughout the years have faced many domestic and international challenges in ensuring the prosperity and security of the United States.

GEORGE
WASHINGTON

1st ★ 1789-1797

George Washington was a military officer who became famous for leading the Continental Army to victory against the British. Known as the "Father of the Country," he played a vital role in drafting the US Constitution. His refusal to take sides in political disputes made him an obvious choice for the first president, and he remains the only president to have been elected unanimously. A unifying figure with no political affiliation, Washington also agreed to several treaties with Britain and France to avoid US involvement in foreign wars.

Presidents

CROSSING THE DELAWARE
This painting by Emanuel Leutze, *Washington Crossing the Delaware*, gives the artist's view of Washington leading his soldiers across the icy Delaware River on Christmas Day, 1776. (In reality, he would never have been so dangerously perched at the front of the boat.) The attack took the British by surprise, and they were defeated at the Battle of Trenton.

DATA FILE

BORN: February 22, 1732, Westmoreland County, Virginia
DIED: December 14, 1799

INAUGURATED AS PRESIDENT:
April 30, 1789, age 57

KEY DATES:

1775 Becomes commander of the Continental Army.

1781 Defeats the British at Yorktown, ending the American Revolution.

1787 Is the first person to sign the United States Constitution.

1793 Begins his second term as president. The Constitution does not specify whether a president can do so, so his actions set a precedent.

1797 Retires to his plantation in Virginia.

☞ Martha Washington **pp.126–127**

☞ The American Revolution **p.148**

☞ The Drafting of the Constitution **pp.150–151**

Washington's second **inaugural address** is the **shortest** given by any president—just **135 words**.

George Washington

REVIEWING THE TROOPS
George Washington reviews the troops gathered at Fort Cumberland, Maryland, on October 18, 1794, before their march to put down the Whiskey Rebellion.

WHISKEY REBELLION

In 1791, to help pay off a large national debt, Washington introduced a new federal tax on distilled spirits, including whiskey. Farmers in Pennsylvania protested and hundreds of armed rebels attacked federal officers. In August 1794, Washington led an army of 15,000 militiamen to enforce this tax. As the army marched into Pennsylvania, the rebels melted away. The tax was abolished in 1801.

Rebels would **cover tax collectors** in **tar and feathers** during the **Whiskey Rebellion**.

George Washington

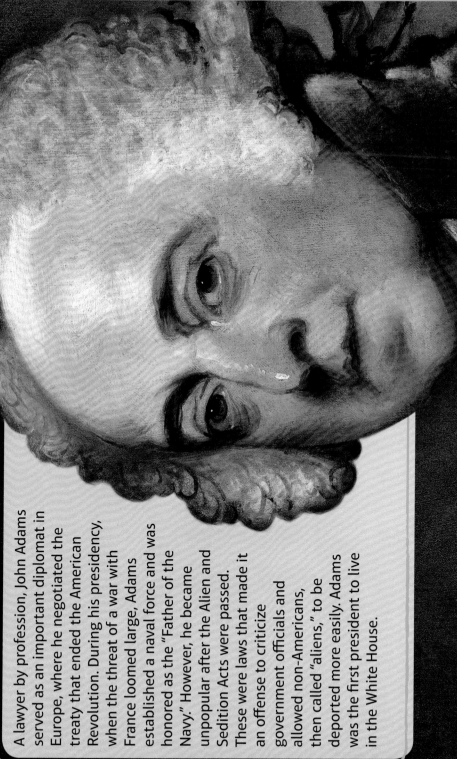

JOHN
ADAMS
2nd ★ 1797–1801

Federalist

A lawyer by profession, John Adams served as an important diplomat in Europe, where he negotiated the treaty that ended the American Revolution. During his presidency, when the threat of a war with France loomed large, Adams established a naval force and was honored as the "Father of the Navy." However, he became unpopular after the Alien and Sedition Acts were passed. These were laws that made it an offense to criticize government officials and allowed non-Americans, then called "aliens," to be deported more easily. Adams was the first president to live in the White House.

BORN: October 30, 1735, Braintree (now Quincy), Massachusetts
DIED: July 4, 1826

INAUGURATED AS PRESIDENT:
March 4, 1797, age 61

KEY DATES:

1776 Serves on the commission that drafts the Declaration of Independence.

1789 Becomes the first vice president of the United States.

1798 Establishes the United States Department of the Navy.

1798 Passes the Alien and Sedition Acts.

1800 Moves into the newly finished White House in Washington, D.C.

☞ Abigail Adams **p.128**

☞ The Declaration of Independence **p.149**

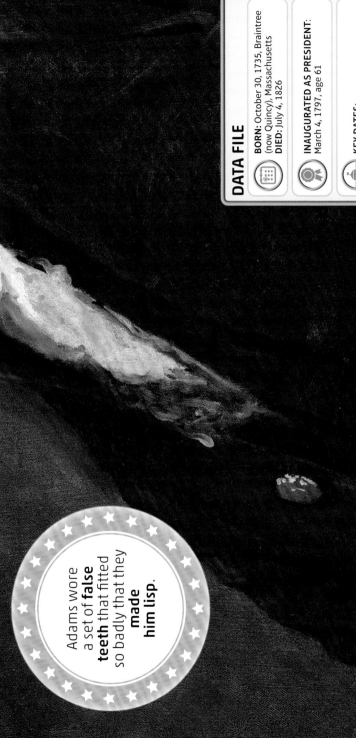

THE XYZ AFFAIR

In 1797, the French foreign minister sent three agents to demand a large bribe from an American peace mission in Paris. To prove what had happened, a furious Adams released documents in which the Frenchmen were referred to as "X, Y, and Z." This British cartoon mocks the event, showing Frenchmen stealing from a woman representing America, while other countries look on.

Adams wore a set of **false teeth** that fitted so badly that they **made him lisp**.

John Adams

THOMAS JEFFERSON

3rd ★ 1801–1809   *Democratic-Republican*

A gifted scholar and lawyer, Thomas Jefferson was the main author of the Declaration of Independence and the first US Secretary of State. As president, he reduced the national debt, but made himself unpopular by forbidding foreign trade to avoid becoming involved in the war between France and Britain.

DATA FILE

 BORN: April 13, 1743, Goochland (now Albemarle) County, Virginia
DIED: July 4, 1826

 INAUGURATED AS PRESIDENT: March 4, 1801, age 57

 KEY DATES:

1776	Drafts the Declaration of Independence.
1801	Becomes the first president to be inaugurated in Washington, D.C., the new federal capital.
1807	Signs the Embargo Act forbidding trade with foreign powers. It is unpopular with businesses and farmers, and is repealed in 1809.
1819	Establishes the University of Virginia.

 The Declaration of Independence **p.149**

Jefferson's **6,500-volume library** became the core collection of the **Library of Congress**.

Presidents

16

SALUTING THE FLAG
Soldiers in New Orleans fire a salute as the American flag is raised and the French flag lowered after the Louisiana Purchase.

THE LOUISIANA PURCHASE

In 1803, Jefferson seized the opportunity to acquire Louisiana from the French Emperor Napoleon for $15 million. It was a vast area of 828,000 sq miles (2,144,510 sq km), which stretched from New Orleans to Montana. This doubled the size of the United States and opened up the territories to the west.

Thomas Jefferson

A NATIVE GUIDE

During their two-year-long journey, Lewis and Clark came across many Indigenous Peoples of North America. Sacagawea, a Shoshone woman whom they met in Dakota, became their interpreter and helped them establish peaceful relations with the Indigenous Peoples they met.

THE LEWIS AND CLARK EXPEDITION

After the Louisiana Purchase, Jefferson decided to send an expedition to explore the new territory. It was led by Meriwether Lewis, Jefferson's private secretary, and William Clark, a former army officer. The Corps of Discovery, as the expedition became known, set out from Missouri in May 1804. They did not find a river route from the US to the Pacific Ocean, as Jefferson had hoped for, but managed to cross the Rocky Mountains and reach the ocean nonetheless. During this journey, the group kept a detailed account of the plants and animals they saw, and made extensive maps of the lands they crossed.

Thomas Jefferson

JAMES MADISON

4th ★ 1809–1817   *Democratic-Republican*

James Madison was popularly known as the "Father of the Constitution." He believed the government should have only the powers granted to it by the Constitution. Madison played a key role in introducing the Bill of Rights, which amended the Constitution and further secured the rights of citizens. His presidency was dominated by growing tensions with Britain and the war that then ensued.

DATA FILE

BORN: March 16, 1751, Port Conway, Virginia
DIED: June 28, 1836

INAUGURATED AS PRESIDENT:
March 4, 1809, age 57

KEY DATES:

1787 Begins writing the Federalist Papers, a series of essays that urged New York voters to ratify the Constitution.

1812 **JUNE 18** Issues a declaration of war against Britain.

 Dolley Madison **p.129**

 The Drafting of the Constitution **pp.150–151**

 The Bill of Rights **pp.158–159**

Extremely rare today, the **$5,000 bill**, issued until 1969, features a **portrait of Madison.**

THE WAR OF 1812

In 1812, a powerful group of young politicians, called the "War Hawks," strongly urged Madison to declare war on Britain. They wanted to stop British ships from harassing American vessels and to take land in Canada, which was still a British colony. Reluctantly, Madison gave in and a military conflict ensued. Although the Americans were initially able to repel British ships, they made little progress advancing into Canada. In 1814, British troops occupied Washington and burned the White House. Later that year, the two sides signed a peace treaty at Ghent, in Belgium, to end the war.

BATTLE OF NEW ORLEANS
Andrew Jackson (on horseback) is shown leading the defense of New Orleans against the British in January 1815. Although the Americans won this battle, it took place two weeks after a peace treaty had been signed, as news traveled slowly at the time.

James Madison

JAMES MONROE

5th ★ 1817–1825   *Democratic-Republican*

James Monroe's extensive political experience as governor of Virginia prepared him well for the presidency. During his first term, he expanded the country with the acquisition of Florida from Spain. He also had to deal with the issue of slavery, which was permitted in the Southern states but had been abolished in the north. When Missouri wanted to join the Union as a slave state, Monroe signed a compromise bill, which stated that the number of slave-holding and free states should be equal. During his second term, Monroe issued a bold policy called the "Monroe Doctrine," in which the United States declared its opposition to any European interference in North and South America, and in exchange the US pledged to stay out of European wars.

Monroe **died on July 4**—the **third president** to have died **on that date**.

MANY YEARS OF SERVICE
By the time Monroe's presidency drew to an end, he had served the United States for 50 years—holding more government offices than any president before or after him. He is pictured here as a young man, but Monroe was 58 years old when he became president.

DATA FILE

BORN: April 28, 1758, Westmoreland County, Virginia
DIED: July 4, 1831

INAUGURATED AS PRESIDENT: March 4, 1817, age 58

KEY DATES:

1799   Serves as governor of Virginia.

1811   Appointed as Secretary of State.

1814   Serves as Secretary of War.

1819   Purchases Florida from Spain for $5 million. This becomes a territory of the US, with its own government, but is not admitted as a state until 1845.

1820   Signs the Missouri Compromise, which admits Missouri to the Union as a slave state, but also admits Maine as a free state.

1823   Announces the Monroe Doctrine in his annual message to Congress.

James Monroe

JOHN QUINCY ADAMS

6th ★ 1825–1829   *Democratic-Republican*

The son of former president John Adams, John Quincy Adams was the first president whose father had also held the same office. In his early career, he was a successful diplomat and served as an ambassador to several European countries before becoming Secretary of State. In this position, he played a key role in negotiating the Adams-Onis Treaty with Spain, which gave the United States control over Florida. After becoming president, Adams proposed the building of new roads and canals. However, he had weak political backing and his plans gained little support.

> **"**The sun of **my political life** sets in the deepest **gloom**. But that of **my country shines** unclouded.**"**

DEATH IN THE HOUSE

After losing the 1828 presidential election, Adams returned to politics as a representative for Massachusetts. He became the only former president to enter Congress, where he had a long career. In 1848, while seated in the House Chamber, Adams suffered a stroke, and died two days later.

DATA FILE

BORN: July 11, 1767, Braintree (now Quincy), Massachusetts
DIED: February 23, 1848

INAUGURATED AS PRESIDENT: March 4, 1825, age 57

KEY DATES:

1819   Negotiates the Adams-Onis Treaty with Spain.

1825   Chosen to be president by the House of Representatives because no candidate had gained a clear majority of the Electoral College votes.

1828   **MAY 19** Signs a bill that increases the tax paid by importers. It becomes known as the "Tariff of Abominations."

John Quincy Adams

ANDREW JACKSON

7th ★ 1829–1837   *Democrat*

An iconic war hero, Andrew Jackson was the first president to be elected for the newly formed Democratic party. His politics, called "Jacksonian Democracy," aimed to defend the rights of ordinary American citizens. Nicknamed "Old Hickory" for his toughness, Jackson threatened to send troops to South Carolina when the state refused to impose a high tariff (tax on imported goods). He also ordered the enforcement of the Indian Removal Act, which led to the Trail of Tears. Between 1830 and 1839, nearly 59,000 Cherokee, Creek, Choctaw, Chickasaw, and Seminole people were forcibly removed from their homelands, and between 8,700 and 17,000 people died. In 1835, he became the first president to suffer an assassination attempt, but escaped unharmed by beating his attacker off with his walking cane.

Presidents

PRESIDENTIAL INAUGURATION

Jackson was inaugurated as president on the East Portico of the United States Capitol building. The White House was opened for a reception afterward, but the crowd grew so large and rowdy that they destroyed furniture and china, and Jackson himself had to be led away for his safety.

DATA FILE

BORN: March 15, 1767, Waxhaw Settlement, South Carolina
DIED: June 8, 1845

INAUGURATED AS PRESIDENT: March 4, 1829, age 61

KEY DATES:

1815 Leads his troops to victory against the British Army in the Battle of New Orleans.

1830 Signs the Indian Removal Act.

1832 Asks Congress for authority to send troops to South Carolina, which had refused to impose a high tariff on imported goods.

1832 Vetoes a bill to set up the Second Bank of the United States, claiming that the bank is unconstitutional.

After being **shot** in a **duel**, Jackson had a **bullet lodged** in his **chest** for **40 years**.

Andrew Jackson

MARTIN VAN BUREN

8th ★ 1837-1841   *Democrat*

Born into a struggling family of Dutch descent, Martin Van Buren was the only president not to speak English as his first language. He could not afford to go to college but studied law independently before entering politics. He spent much of his presidency dealing with a severe economic recession, although his budget cuts made this worse. Van Buren also opposed the extension of slavery to new states, blocking Texas from joining the Union as a slave state.

DATA FILE

 BORN: December 5, 1782, Kinderhook, New York
DIED: July 24, 1862

 INAUGURATED AS PRESIDENT: March 4, 1837, age 54

 KEY DATES:

1837 Calls for a special session of Congress in response to the Panic of 1837, which had caused an economic depression.

1839 Prevents war between militias in Maine and the Canadian province of New Brunswick over a border dispute.

1840 Signs the Independent Treasury Act, which separates government funds from private banks. Van Buren proposed this act due to the recession earlier in his term, which was caused by the banks.

The word "okay" originates from Van Buren's nickname "Old Kinderhook."

THE TRAIL OF TEARS

The Indian Removal Act of 1830 allowed the president to remove Indigenous Peoples of North America west of the Mississippi River in order to acquire their lands in the southeast. The Seminole, Creek, Choctaw and Chickasaw were removed against their will, but the Cherokees fought against their removal in court. However, in 1836, a treaty was forced upon them and they were given two years to leave their lands. In November 1838, Van Buren sent federal troops to force them westward. Around 4,000 Cherokee died during this harrowing journey, known as the Trail of Tears, falling victim to harsh weather, disease, and lack of food.

LEAVING THEIR HOME

In the painting below, Cherokee families are shown along the "Trail of Tears." Their 1,000-mile (1,600-km) journey to Oklahoma took them through the worst of a severe winter.

Martin Van Buren

WILLIAM HENRY
HARRISON

9th ★ March–April 1841   *Whig*

A celebrated war hero, William Henry Harrison won the nickname "Old Tip" after he defeated Indigenous Chief Tecumseh at the Battle of Tippecanoe Creek. Having had a successful career in the army, he entered politics, and went on to became the governor of the Indiana Territory. Harrison later stood for two presidential elections, winning in 1840 and becoming the first president from the Whig party. However, he soon caught a severe cold that led to a fatal bout of pneumonia. Harrison died a month later, becoming the shortest-serving president in the history of the United States.

Harrison's **inaugural address** was the **longest** ever, at 1 hour and 45 minutes.

DATA FILE

BORN: February 9, 1773, Berkeley, Virginia
DIED: April 4, 1841

INAUGURATED AS PRESIDENT: March 4, 1841, age 68

KEY DATES:

1791 Joins the army as a junior commissioned officer.

1798 Begins his early political career, becoming secretary of the Northwest Territory.

1800 Becomes governor of the Indiana Territory.

1811 Defeats the Shawnee chief Tecumseh at the Battle of Tippecanoe Creek.

1840 Wins the presidential election with 234 Electoral College votes to Martin Van Buren's 60.

Political Parties **pp.200–201**

WHIG PROPAGANDA

During the election of 1840, Harrison's Whig party portrayed him as a simple man, brought up in a log cabin. They made posters such as this one, showing him greeting fellow war veterans, in order to contrast him with his luxury-loving opponent. The propaganda worked, and Harrison—in fact from a wealthy Virginia family— won easily.

William Henry Harrison

JOHN TYLER

10th ★ 1841–1845 ★ Whig until 1842

When John Tyler became the president after much debate, it set a precedent for vice presidents to become president upon the death of their predecessor. Tyler's views did not align with those of the Whig party. He supported states' rights, including their right to protect slavery. During his time in office, he vetoed a bill to set up a national bank, although his party supported it. As a result, he was expelled from the Whigs and spent most of his term party-less. He was not chosen as their candidate in the 1844 election, but won a seat in the Confederate Congress in 1861.

Tyler was the father of **15 children**— the **most** of any president.

THE ANNEXATION OF TEXAS

After a lengthy military conflict, Texas declared itself independent from Mexico in 1836. Because it had a large number of American settlers, many Texans wanted to join the United States and Tyler supported them, annexing the state in 1845. Here, the Texas flag flies over the Alamo (a famous battle site) in celebration.

DATA FILE

BORN: March 29, 1790, Charles City County, Virginia
DIED: January 18, 1862

INAUGURATED AS PRESIDENT:
April 6, 1841, age 51

KEY DATES:

1841 Vetoes a bill to set up a national bank. This leads to his entire Cabinet resigning.

1842 Expelled from the Whig Party. Remains party-less for most of his term.

1844 Marries Julia Gardiner and becomes the first president to get married while in office.

1845 Signs bills admitting Florida and Texas into the Union as the 27th and 28th states.

John Tyler

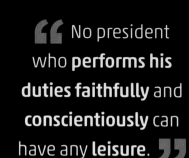

JAMES K.
POLK
11th ★ 1845–1849　　　　*Democrat*

Previously the governor of Tennessee, James K. Polk was relatively unknown when he ran for office. He believed in the theory of "Manifest Destiny," the idea that the United States was destined to expand across North America, and he promised to complete the annexation of Texas, settle the dispute with Britain over the boundaries of Oregon, and acquire land in California from Mexico. As president, Polk achieved all these aims, and captained a great territorial expansion of the United States. He decided not to run for a second term, and stepped down in 1849.

DATA FILE

 BORN: November 2, 1795, Mecklenburg County, North Carolina
DIED: June 15, 1849

 INAUGURATED AS PRESIDENT: March 4, 1845, age 49

 KEY DATES:

1825　Elected to the House of Representatives.

1846　**MAY 13** Signs a declaration of war against Mexico.

1846　Signs a bill reducing import tariffs to low levels and another establishing local subtreasuries to manage federal funds.

       No president who **performs his duties faithfully** and **conscientiously** can have any **leisure**.

THE MEXICAN-AMERICAN WAR

Although Texas had been annexed, there continued to be disagreement between the United States and Mexico over the southern border of the state. In 1846, Polk sent General Zachary Taylor and his troops to the disputed area. When the Mexicans attacked the American forces, war was declared. General Taylor won several victories against the Mexicans, even capturing additional land in Mexico. In 1848, the Treaty of Guadalupe Hidalgo was signed, which made the river, Rio Grande, the boundary between Texas and Mexico and gave the United States additional land in California and New Mexico.

BATTLE OF RESACA DE LA PALMA
United States cavalry units are shown charging the Mexican army at the Battle of Resaca de la Palma on May 9, 1846. General Zachary Taylor's victory forced the Mexican troops to retreat south of the Rio Grande river.

James K. Polk

ZACHARY TAYLOR

12th ★ 1849–1850

Whig

A career army officer, Zachary Taylor's success as one of the commanders in the Mexican-American War of 1846 made him a war hero. Nicknamed "Old Rough and Ready" for his willingness to get things done, he was highly popular and won the 1848 election despite his lack of political experience. Although he was a slave owner himself, Taylor discouraged the extension of slavery to new territories and states. He tried to hold the Union together by opposing the Compromise of 1850, which would permit federal territories in the west (areas owned by the United States but not officially recognized as states), such as Utah, to allow slavery. Taylor became ill and died five days after attending a sweltering July 4 ceremony.

Taylor kept his **former war horse, "Old Whitey,"** on the front **lawn of the White House.**

DATA FILE

BORN: November 24, 1784, Orange County, Virginia
DIED: July 9, 1850

INAUGURATED AS PRESIDENT: March 4, 1849, age 64

KEY DATES:

1812 Serves in the army in the War of 1812.

1847 Defeats a large Mexican force at Buena Vista during the Mexican-American War.

1850 **APRIL** Signs the Clayton-Bulwer Treaty with Britain, agreeing to join together to build and guard a canal across Central America.

1850 **JULY** Threatens to veto the Compromise of 1850, but dies before he can do so.

Zachary Taylor

MILLARD FILLMORE

13th ★ 1850-1853   *Whig*

Born to a poor farming family, Millard Fillmore was a self-taught lawyer whose presidency began unexpectedly when President Taylor died. The issue of slavery dominated his time in office, and he supported the Compromise of 1850. This allowed California to become a free state, but also permitted slavery in Utah and New Mexico. It also included signing the Fugitive Slave Act that sanctioned the pursuit and recapture of escaped slaves in free northern territories. His actions outraged the Northerners and widened the gap between the free and slave states. This helped to bring an end to the Whig Party.

Fillmore began **formal school** at the **age of 19**, and ended up **marrying** his **teacher**.

DATA FILE

BORN: January 7, 1800, Cayuga County, New York
DIED: March 8, 1874

INAUGURATED AS PRESIDENT: July 10, 1850, age 50

KEY DATES:

1832   Elected to the House of Representatives.

1850   **AUGUST** Sends 750 federal troops to stop the state of Texas from invading New Mexico over a border issue.

1850   **SEPTEMBER** Signs the Compromise of 1850, including the Fugitive Slave Act, which made the federal government responsible for catching and returning runaways.

PERRY'S MISSION TO JAPAN

Fillmore wanted to establish a trade link with Japan, which had refused to trade with foreign powers for more than 200 years. In 1853, he sent Commodore Matthew Perry with a fleet of four ships to visit Japan. The mission led to the opening of Japanese ports to American ships and four years later, a trade agreement between the two countries was signed.

Millard Fillmore

FRANKLIN PIERCE

14th ★ 1853-1857   *Democrat*

Having previously served as both a representative and senator, Franklin Pierce was elected president in 1852 when the Democrats could not agree between four other contenders. His presidency was overshadowed by the debate over whether to allow slavery in Kansas. A supporter of westward expansion, he promoted the Gadsden Purchase by which the United States acquired land that became parts of modern-day Arizona and New Mexico. He also threatened war against Spain if it did not sell Cuba to the United States.

DATA FILE

 BORN: November 23, 1804, Hillsboro, New Hampshire
DIED: October 8, 1869

 INAUGURATED AS PRESIDENT: March 4, 1853, age 48

 KEY DATES:

1847 Serves in the army during the Mexican-American War.

1854 **APRIL** Signs the treaty authorizing the Gadsden Purchase, which acquires land from Mexico for $10 million.

1854 Issues the Ostend Manifesto, which threatens to take Cuba from Spain by force.

Pierce gave his **3,319-word inaugural** address from **memory**—with **no notes**.

THE KANSAS-NEBRASKA ACT

In 1854, Pierce signed the Kansas-Nebraska Act, allowing each of the two territories to decide if they wanted to enter the Union as slave states (states where slavery was permitted). The Act opposed the Missouri Compromise of 1820, which banned slavery in the region. It reignited the disagreement between the proslavery and antislavery forces in Kansas, and led to a period of political chaos and bloodshed, known as Bleeding Kansas. In 1861, Kansas finally joined as a free state.

BORDER RUFFIANS

Thousands of proslavery settlers, called "Border Ruffians," streamed into Kansas after the Kansas-Nebraska Act. They wanted to make sure that Kansas became a slave state and clashed violently with "Free Staters," who opposed this.

Franklin Pierce

JAMES BUCHANAN

15th ★ 1857–1861

Democrat

Known as "Old Buck," James Buchanan was 65 when he was elected and had a wealth of political experience behind him. However, like his predecessors, much of his presidency was spent dealing with growing tensions over the issue of slavery. He supported the Dred Scott decision by the Supreme Court, which ruled that Black people were not citizens, and was also in favor of allowing Kansas to be admitted as a slave state. This made him popular in the South, but growing abolitionist demands in the North led Southern politicians to believe no compromise was possible. By the end of his term, seven Southern states had left the Union.

Buchanan is the **only president** to have **never** been **married**.

JOHN BROWN'S RAID

On October 16, 1859, John Brown led a group of 22 abolitionists in an attack on the federal armory at Harpers Ferry, Virginia. The group wanted to use the weapons stored there to free enslaved people and kick-start a rebellion. Buchanan sent US marines to fight the raiders, and Brown's plan failed. Although some Northerners praised his actions, Brown was the first person ever to be executed for treason in the United States.

DATA FILE

BORN: April 23, 1791, Cove Gap, Pennsylvania
DIED: June 1, 1868

INAUGURATED AS PRESIDENT: March 4, 1857, age 65

KEY DATES:

1820 Elected to the House of Representatives.

1857 Promotes the Lecompton Constitution, which supported admitting Kansas to the Union as a slave state.

1866 Publishes the first presidential memoir, *Mr. Buchanan's Administration on the Eve of the Rebellion*.

James Buchanan

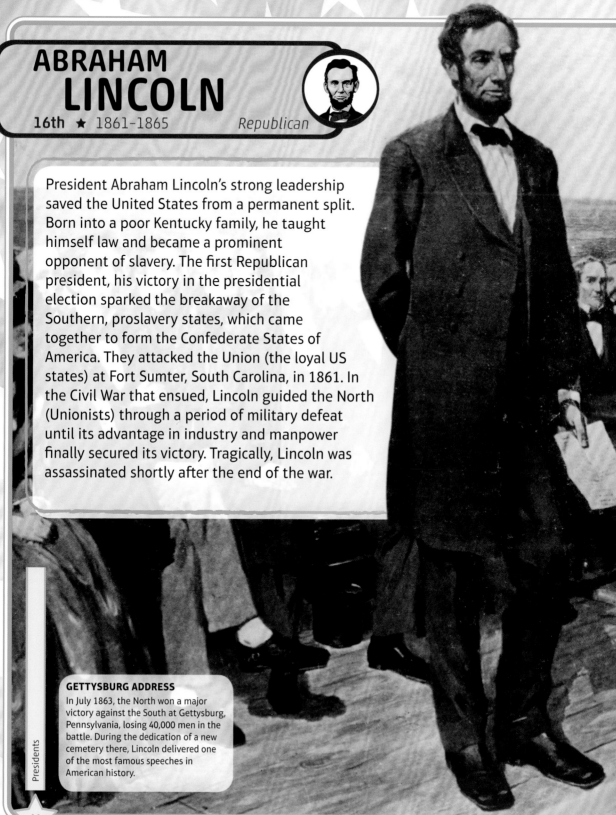

ABRAHAM LINCOLN

16th ★ 1861–1865   *Republican*

President Abraham Lincoln's strong leadership saved the United States from a permanent split. Born into a poor Kentucky family, he taught himself law and became a prominent opponent of slavery. The first Republican president, his victory in the presidential election sparked the breakaway of the Southern, proslavery states, which came together to form the Confederate States of America. They attacked the Union (the loyal US states) at Fort Sumter, South Carolina, in 1861. In the Civil War that ensued, Lincoln guided the North (Unionists) through a period of military defeat until its advantage in industry and manpower finally secured its victory. Tragically, Lincoln was assassinated shortly after the end of the war.

GETTYSBURG ADDRESS

In July 1863, the North won a major victory against the South at Gettysburg, Pennsylvania, losing 40,000 men in the battle. During the dedication of a new cemetery there, Lincoln delivered one of the most famous speeches in American history.

Presidents

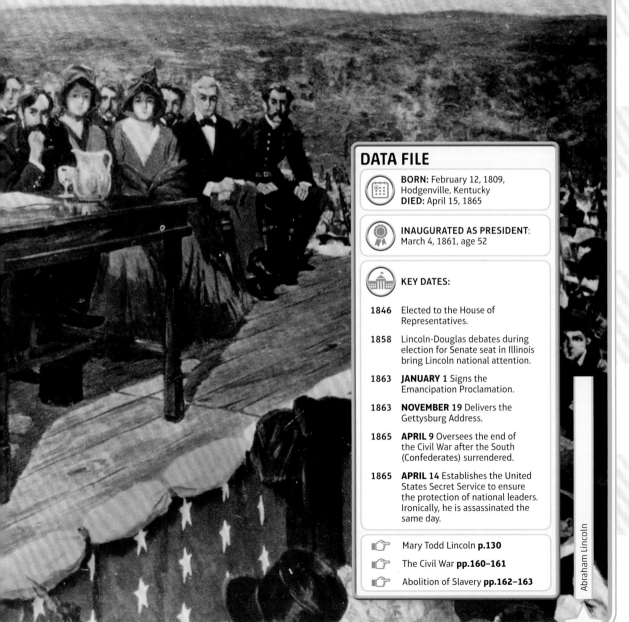

> **We here highly resolve** that these **dead** shall **not** have **died in vain**, that this **nation under God** shall have a **new birth of freedom**, and that **government of the people**, by the people, **for the people** shall **not perish** from the **earth.**
>
> Abraham Lincoln, Gettysburg Address

DATA FILE

BORN: February 12, 1809, Hodgenville, Kentucky
DIED: April 15, 1865

INAUGURATED AS PRESIDENT: March 4, 1861, age 52

KEY DATES:

1846 Elected to the House of Representatives.

1858 Lincoln-Douglas debates during election for Senate seat in Illinois bring Lincoln national attention.

1863 **JANUARY 1** Signs the Emancipation Proclamation.

1863 **NOVEMBER 19** Delivers the Gettysburg Address.

1865 **APRIL 9** Oversees the end of the Civil War after the South (Confederates) surrendered.

1865 **APRIL 14** Establishes the United States Secret Service to ensure the protection of national leaders. Ironically, he is assassinated the same day.

☞ Mary Todd Lincoln **p.130**

☞ The Civil War **pp.160–161**

☞ Abolition of Slavery **pp.162–163**

Abraham Lincoln

THE EMANCIPATION PROCLAMATION

On January 1, 1863, Lincoln issued the Emancipation Proclamation. It declared all enslaved people in the breakaway Confederate states to be free, and allowed free Black men to join the Union army. Lincoln hoped this would increase his support among Northern abolitionists and encourage enslaved people in the South to escape and flee to the North.

LINCOLN AND SLAVERY

Lincoln expressed antislavery sentiments throughout his life, but struggled with how to address slavery as president. Here he receives prominent antislavery campaigner Sojourner Truth into the White House in 1864, over a year after the Emancipation Proclamation was signed.

ASSASSINATION

On April 14, 1865, five days after the Civil War ended, Lincoln was enjoying a play at Ford's Theatre, in Washington, D.C. During the third act, John Wilkes Booth, a Confederate supporter, sneaked into the private box where the president was seated and shot him in the back of his head. Lincoln was carried across the street to a boarding house, where he died the following morning.

DEATH AT THE THEATRE
Booth entered Lincoln's box while the presidential bodyguard was away. The single bullet he shot was fatal.

ANDREW JOHNSON

17th ★ 1865–1869 · *Democrat*

Andrew Johnson had been vice president just six weeks when Lincoln was assassinated. He was a Southerner and a Democrat who supported states' rights. This led him to be lenient toward the Southern states during the Reconstruction period after the Civil War, pardoning all who would take an oath of allegiance to the Union. However, the Radical Republicans opposed this approach and passed legislation protecting the rights of formerly enslaved people, overturning Johnson's veto on several occasions.

Johnson's **parents** were **illiterate** and it was **his wife** who **taught** him how to **read and write**.

DATA FILE

BORN: December 29, 1808, Raleigh, North Carolina
DIED: July 31, 1875

INAUGURATED AS PRESIDENT:
April 15, 1865, age 56

 KEY DATES:

1843   Elected to the House of Representatives.

1867   Sends Secretary of State William Seward to negotiate the purchase of Alaska from Russia.

1868   Acquitted in his impeachment trial.

 Abolition of Slavery **pp.162–163**

IMPEACHMENT

Throughout his presidency, Johnson repeatedly clashed with the Republican-dominated Congress, leading them to pass several acts limiting his presidential powers. In 1867, Johnson defied one of these by removing the Secretary of War approved by the Senate and selecting his own candidate. Furious at his actions, the House of Representatives voted to impeach the president, which would bring formal charges against Johnson and could remove him from office. The trial went to the Senate, which eventually ruled in Johnson's favor by just one vote.

SERVING THE SUMMONS
Andrew Johnson was handed a summons on March 7, 1868, ordering him to appear before the Senate. He remains one of only three presidents to be impeached by Congress.

Andrew Johnson

ULYSSES S. GRANT

18th ★ 1869-1877   *Republican*

One of the Union's best generals in the Civil War, Ulysses S. Grant was renowned for leading the United States to victory over the Confederate states. A war hero from humble origins, his popularity helped him win the 1868 presidential election. However, he came into office during a difficult time in American history, faced with economic problems and the Reconstruction of the South. Grant favored mild measures to bring the last three states—Mississippi, Texas, and Virginia—back into the Union. However, he eventually threatened force against those states that denied the vote to Black people. He was elected for a second term, but this was plagued by scandals, which tarnished his popularity.

DATA FILE

BORN: April 27, 1822, Point Pleasant, Ohio
DIED: July 23, 1885

INAUGURATED AS PRESIDENT: March 4, 1869, age 46

KEY DATES:

1870   Helps pass the 15th Amendment, which forbids denying rights to American citizens on the basis of their race.

1870   Helps pass the Naturalization Act which grants citizenship to people born in Africa or of African descent.

 The Civil War **pp.160–161**

 Voting Rights **pp.164–165**

A **$50 bill** is **nicknamed** a **"Grant"** because it has his **portrait** on it.

THE PANIC OF 1873

In September 1873, Jay Cooke and Company, a bank with major investments in railroads, declared bankruptcy. This set off a series of other bank failures, and soon a major economic panic had swept the nation. Grant's policies were ineffective in stopping this and mass unemployment and strikes followed.

Ulysses S. Grant

RUTHERFORD B. HAYES

19th ★ **1877-1881**　　*Republican*

A strong abolitionist who defended runaway enslaved people in court before becoming governor of Ohio, Rutherford B. Hayes was a well-liked presidential candidate within his party. He lost the popular vote only to win the Electoral College after Congress awarded him 20 contested votes in the Compromise of 1877. As president, he oversaw the final stage of Reconstruction and withdrew the federal army from the South. He had strained relations with Congress, which blocked his plans to reform the Civil Service.

DATA FILE

 BORN: October 4, 1822, Delaware, Ohio
DIED: January 17, 1893

 INAUGURATED AS PRESIDENT:
March 4, 1877, age 55

 KEY DATES:

1861 Wounded five times while serving in the Union Army in the Civil War, and is promoted for bravery in battle.

1877 Orders the last federal troops to leave the Southern states.

1877 Issues an order barring all federal employees from political activity in an attempt to begin reforming the Civil Service.

 The Civil War **pp.160–161**

 Extraordinary Elections **pp.196–197**

In **1878,** Hayes **began** the tradition of the **Easter Egg roll** on the **White House lawn**.

CHINESE EXCLUSION ACT

Chinese immigration to the US had been constant since the 1850s, with many immigrants working on the railroads. However, they were racially discriminated against and paid poor wages while enduring grueling physical labor. Resentful of "too many" Chinese looking for work, Congress passed a bill forbidding all Chinese immigration. Hayes, however, vetoed the bill, which went against the terms of an earlier treaty with China. Instead, he negotiated a new agreement, which allowed immigration, but at a reduced rate. Sadly, the Chinese Exclusion Act was revived once Hayes left office, and the struggle for equality continued for many decades.

DIPLOMATIC MEETING
President Hayes is shown here meeting Chinese diplomats during the negotiations for the new treaty.

Rutherford B. Hayes

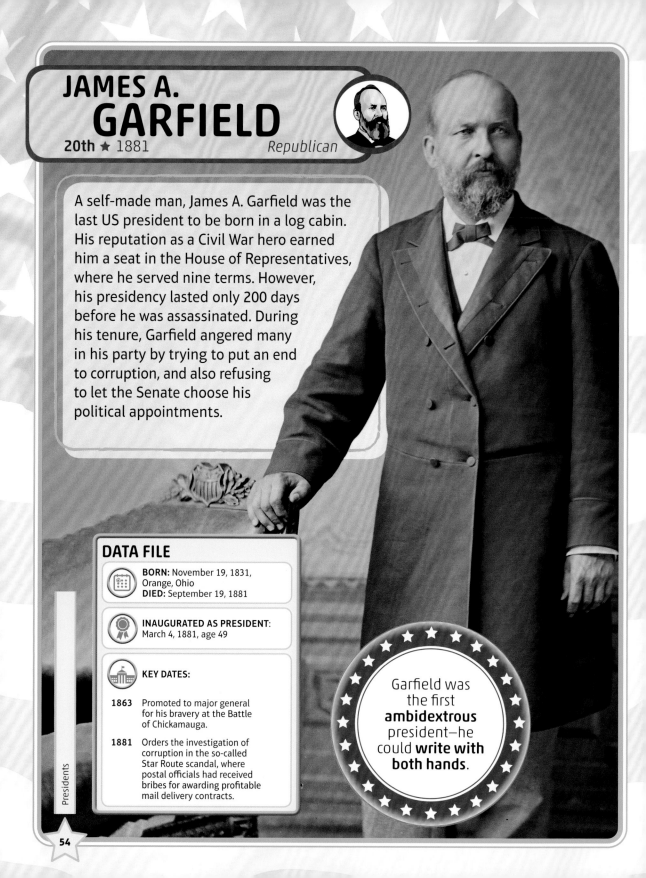

JAMES A. GARFIELD

20th ★ 1881   *Republican*

A self-made man, James A. Garfield was the last US president to be born in a log cabin. His reputation as a Civil War hero earned him a seat in the House of Representatives, where he served nine terms. However, his presidency lasted only 200 days before he was assassinated. During his tenure, Garfield angered many in his party by trying to put an end to corruption, and also refusing to let the Senate choose his political appointments.

DATA FILE

BORN: November 19, 1831, Orange, Ohio
DIED: September 19, 1881

INAUGURATED AS PRESIDENT:
March 4, 1881, age 49

KEY DATES:

1863   Promoted to major general for his bravery at the Battle of Chickamauga.

1881   Orders the investigation of corruption in the so-called Star Route scandal, where postal officials had received bribes for awarding profitable mail delivery contracts.

Garfield was the first **ambidextrous** president—he could **write with both hands**.

ASSASSINATION

Following his support of Civil Service reform, President Garfield was shot by Charles Guiteau, a delusional, disaffected supporter, on July 2, 1881. The president was severely wounded and was taken back to the White House. He underwent treatment for two months. The dirty instruments used to treat the wound caused blood poisoning, and Garfield died on September 19.

BITTER ATTACK
Garfield's attacker, Charles Guiteau, opened fire at the Baltimore and Potomac Railroad Station in Washington, D.C., while the president was waiting for a train. Guiteau was quickly arrested after the shooting, found guilty at trial, and was hanged on June 30, 1882.

James A. Garfield

CHESTER A. ARTHUR

21st ★ 1881–1885   *Republican*

The son of an immigrant from northern Ireland, Chester A. Arthur proved to be a surprisingly capable president when he assumed office after Garfield's assassination. For years he had benefited from the "spoils system," where political jobs were given to a party's supporters and friends, and Arthur was expected to pack his cabinet with his own supporters. However, he actually introduced reforms that increased the number of jobs awarded on merit.

Arthur was **very particular** about his **clothes** and allegedly **owned 80 pairs of trousers**.

DATA FILE

BORN: October 5, 1830, Fairfield, Vermont
DIED: November 18, 1886

INAUGURATED AS PRESIDENT: September 20, 1881, age 50

KEY DATES:

1882   Signs the Chinese Exclusion Act forbidding immigration from China for 10 years.

1883   Proposes a reduction in tariffs on imports, but Congress adds so many exceptions to it that it becomes known as the "Mongrel Tariff" and is not very successful.

1883   Increases naval funds, so the navy can purchase its first steel vessels.

THE PENDLETON ACT

Until the 1880s, most Civil Service jobs were awarded on the basis of the "spoils system." However, this did not help government departments work efficiently, and in 1883, President Arthur signed the Pendleton Civil Service Reform Act into law. Often referred to as the "Pendleton Act" after its chief sponsor, Senator George Pendleton, this reform created an independent commission to oversee the Civil Service and introduced written examinations for those applying for top government jobs.

BITTERSWEET VICTORY

Although the act was championed by Democrat George Pendleton, it meant that Democrats would no longer be able to remove Republican office holders and replace them with their own. In this cartoon, Pendleton is congratulated by a Republican and realizes he has inadvertently helped his rival party.

Chester A. Arthur

GROVER
CLEVELAND

22nd / 24th ★ 1885–1889 / 1893–1897 *Democrat*

A former governor of New York State, Grover Cleveland is the only president to have served two nonconsecutive terms, and was the first Democrat to be elected after the Civil War. In order to prevent Congress from enacting measures he did not support, Cleveland vetoed more legislation than any other president before him. He also opposed foreign intervention. His second term was hit by an economic recession, which led to his falling popularity.

DATA FILE

 BORN: March 18, 1837, Caldwell, New Jersey
DIED: June 24 1908

 INAUGURATED AS PRESIDENT:
March 4, 1885, age 47
March 4, 1893, age 55

 KEY DATES:

1893 Refuses to advance a treaty that would annex the Hawaii islands.

1893 Repeals the Sherman Silver Purchase Act. This act had required Congress to purchase a mandatory amount of silver each month, and Cleveland blamed it for the recession.

 Frances Cleveland **p.131**

Cleveland **recommended** Congress accept the **Statue of Liberty** as **a gift from France**.

TAKING THE OATH
Cleveland, in the purple suit, places his hand on a Bible as he is sworn in for his first term in office.

THE PULLMAN STRIKE

In 1894, Chicago's Pullman railroad company reduced wages by 30 percent because of the economic crisis. This sparked a nationwide railroad strike that ended in violent clashes when Cleveland sent in federal troops (shown here) to end the strike. The events drew public attention to labor conditions.

Grover Cleveland

BENJAMIN HARRISON

23rd ★ 1889–1893   *Republican*

The grandson of William Henry Harrison—the ninth president—Benjamin Harrison was a Civil War veteran with a reputation for honesty. During his tenure, he raised tariffs on imports to protect American goods, and also pursued an active foreign policy, submitting plans to annex Hawaii. Harrison oversaw the admittance of six new western states to the Union.

Harrison was the **first** president to have **electricity installed** in the **White House**.

DATA FILE

BORN: August 20, 1833, North Bend, Ohio
DIED: March 13, 1901

INAUGURATED AS PRESIDENT: March 4, 1889, age 55

KEY DATES:

1862   Volunteers for the Union army during the Civil War.

1881   Elected to the US Senate.

1890   Signs Sherman Antitrust Act into law, which is aimed at breaking up monopolies.

ENTERING THE HARBOR
For many immigrants arriving from Europe, the Statue of Liberty was their first sight of the United States.

ELLIS ISLAND

Until 1890, immigration policy was the responsibility of individual states. However, during Harrison's presidency the federal government took control. In 1892, a center at Ellis Island, New York City, was opened in which all new arrivals had to be processed. In the first year, 450,000 immigrants arrived, and over 12 million had passed through before Ellis Island was closed in 1954.

Benjamin Harrison

WILLIAM McKINLEY

25th ★ 1897-1901 *Republican*

After 14 years as a US representative, and eight as governor of Ohio, William McKinley aimed to protect the American economy by raising tariffs and linking the US dollar to the value of gold. He was an imperialist who advocated for the expansion of US territories. In 1901, six months into his second term, McKinley was assassinated by an anarchist.

DATA FILE

 BORN: January 29, 1843, Niles, Ohio
DIED: September 14, 1901

 INAUGURATED AS PRESIDENT: March 4, 1897, age 54

 KEY DATES:

1897 Authorizes the Dingley Tariff Act, raising US tariffs to their highest levels.

1898 US annexes Hawaii.

1900 Sends US troops to China to help quell the Boxer Rebellion.

McKinley's **inauguration** in **1897** was the **first to be filmed**.

THE SPANISH-AMERICAN WAR

Cuba had begun fighting for independence from Spain in 1895. After a US battleship mysteriously blew up in Cuba in February 1898, and amid reports of Spanish brutality, McKinley agreed to go to war. US forces easily defeated the Spanish in Cuba, and won naval battles across the Pacific, defeating Spain. In December, the US acquired Puerto Rico, Guam, the Philippines, and Cuba, and awarded Cuba independence.

BATTLE OF MANILA BAY
US Marines watch from the shore as the Spanish fleet is defeated during a battle at Manila in the Philippines, on May 1, 1898. The first major engagement of the war, this battle was a decisive naval victory for the US.

William McKinley

THEODORE ROOSEVELT

26th ★ 1901–1909   *Republican*

Rising unexpectedly to the presidency after McKinley's assassination, Theodore Roosevelt proved to be an able and active leader whose determination to enact change greatly enhanced the reputation of the presidential office. He clamped down on big businesses to stop their unfair practices, pushed for laws to improve the quality of America's food, and established the first national parks in the country. On the international front, he oversaw the building of the Panama Canal, and won the Nobel Peace Prize for negotiating the Treaty of Portsmouth, which ended the war between Russia and Japan. Roosevelt ran for a third term in 1912 under the banner of the Bull Moose Party, splitting the Republican vote and pushing Taft, the incumbent, into third place.

A **boxing accident** left Roosevelt virtually **blind** in his **left eye**.

Presidents

DATA FILE

BORN: October 27, 1858, New York, New York
DIED: January 6, 1919

INAUGURATED AS PRESIDENT: September 14, 1901, age 42

KEY DATES:

1898 Leads a volunteer cavalry regiment called the "Rough Riders" during the Spanish-American War.

1902 Orders action against the Northern Securities Company for unfairly restricting trade.

1906 **JUNE** Signs the Meat Inspection and Pure Food and Drug Acts, beginning government inspection of the food industry.

1906 **DECEMBER** Awarded the Nobel Peace Prize.

Theodore Roosevelt

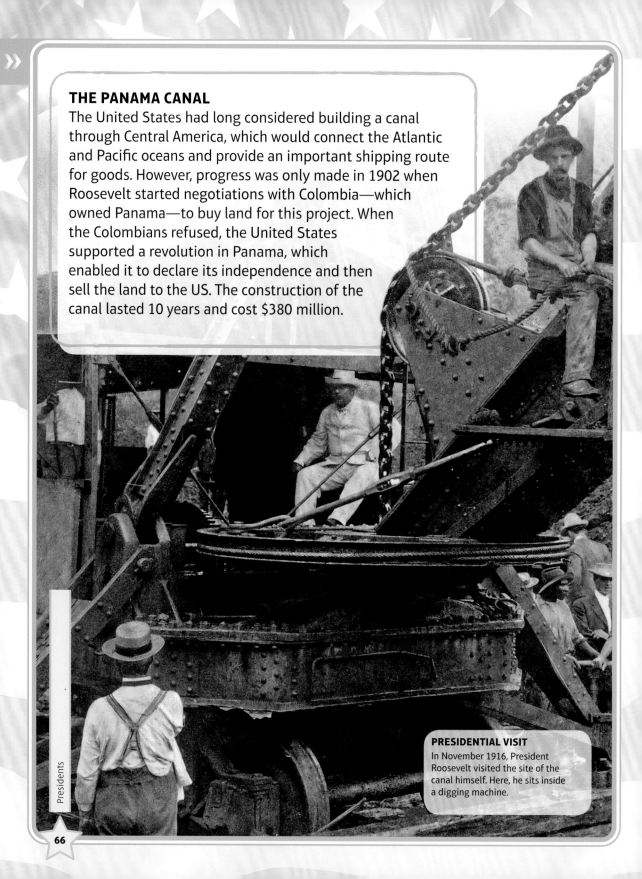

THE PANAMA CANAL

The United States had long considered building a canal through Central America, which would connect the Atlantic and Pacific oceans and provide an important shipping route for goods. However, progress was only made in 1902 when Roosevelt started negotiations with Colombia—which owned Panama—to buy land for this project. When the Colombians refused, the United States supported a revolution in Panama, which enabled it to declare its independence and then sell the land to the US. The construction of the canal lasted 10 years and cost $380 million.

PRESIDENTIAL VISIT
In November 1916, President Roosevelt visited the site of the canal himself. Here, he sits inside a digging machine.

CONSERVATION AND THE RECLAMATION ACT

Roosevelt's concern for the environment earned him the nickname "The Great Conservationist." After his wife and his mother died on the same day in 1884, he retreated for two formative years to North Dakota as a rancher. Through the Reclamation Act of 1902, he secured funds from the sale of lands in the West to build dams to irrigate areas that were too dry for agriculture. Roosevelt also established the National Park Service and added 195,329 sq miles (505,900 sq km) to the national forests.

PROTECTING THE ENVIRONMENT

Roosevelt spent three days on a camping trip in Yosemite National Park with naturalist John Muir. During their trip, Muir persuaded the president to extend the boundaries that were under the park's protection.

Theodore Roosevelt

WILLIAM H. TAFT

27th ★ **1909-1913**   *Republican*

Before becoming president, William H. Taft had gained wide experience as Solicitor General and governor of the Philippines. Trained as a lawyer, he had hoped for a place on the Supreme Court and was a reluctant presidential candidate. Upon taking office, he championed tariff reduction and employed "dollar diplomacy," a policy where the US provided loans to foreign countries in order to increase its overseas influence. With the admission of New Mexico and Arizona to the Union, he became the first president of the "contiguous 48" states.

THE PAYNE-ALDRICH ACT

Named after Senators Sereno E. Payne and Nelson W. Aldrich, the Payne-Aldrich Act was passed in 1909 to lower tariffs on goods entering the United States. However, the bill was weak, and lowered tariffs by only a very small percentage. Many Republicans were angered by Taft's support of it and this cartoon mocks the president, showing him greeting the "crippled" tariff bill.

THE FIRST PITCH

President Taft is shown here with his wife Helen at a baseball game in New York City. Taft began the custom of the president throwing the first pitch at the start of the professional season.

DATA FILE

BORN: September 15, 1857, Cincinnati, Ohio
DIED: March 8, 1930

INAUGURATED AS PRESIDENT: March 4, 1909, age 51

KEY DATES:

1890 Appointed US Solicitor General.

1901 Appointed governor of the Philippines.

1904 Appointed Secretary of War under Theodore Roosevelt.

1921 Appointed Chief Justice of the US Supreme Court.

Taft is the **only person** to hold **both** the positions of **Chief Justice** of the US Supreme Court and that of **US President**.

William H. Taft

WOODROW WILSON

28th ★ 1913-1921   *Democrat*

A former professor and university president, Woodrow Wilson was a capable and determined president. A keen reformer, he pushed for lower tariffs and formed the Federal Trade Commission to clamp down on unfair business practices. When faced with Germany declaring it would resume attacks on US ships, and German attempts to gain Mexican support, Wilson took America into World War I. He later won the Nobel Peace Prize for his involvement in the post-war negotiations.

DATA FILE

 BORN: December 28, 1856, Staunton, Virginia
DIED: February 3, 1924

 INAUGURATED AS PRESIDENT: March 4, 1913, age 56

 KEY DATES:

1890 Appointed as a professor of political science at Princeton University.

1917 Delivers a speech in the Senate urging the countries involved in World War I to opt for "peace without victory."

 Edith Wilson **p.132**

 Prohibition **pp.166–167**

 Female Suffrage **pp.168–169**

Wilson kept a **flock of sheep** on the **White House lawn**.

Presidents

70

THE TREATY OF VERSAILLES

Long before World War I ended, Wilson had drawn up proposals for an international peace settlement, known as the "Fourteen Points." These called for mild measures against the defeated countries and the establishment of a "League of Nations" to promote world peace. However, when the negotiations took place in Versailles, France, in 1919, the European leaders imposed much harsher terms on Germany than Wilson had hoped for. Back home, his plans also fell through when the Senate rejected the Treaty of Versailles and refused to join the League.

THE BIG FOUR

Most of the peace decisions were made by the Big Four nations: Italy, Britain, France, and the US. Here, their leaders, Vittorio Emanuele Orlando, David Lloyd George, Georges Clemenceau, and Wilson are pictured (seated, left to right) during the negotiations.

Woodrow Wilson

WARREN G. HARDING

29th ★ 1921-1923   *Republican*

Having made his fortune as a newspaper publisher, Warren G. Harding was a compromise choice as the Republican presidential candidate in 1920. His appeal for a "return to normalcy" after the war won him the election, but he proved to be a weak leader and was only able to push through a few major changes. He set rules for government spending by establishing the Bureau of the Budget in 1921, but was plagued by a series of corruption scandals, notably the Teapot Dome Scandal, during his time in office. He died suddenly in 1923, before these scandals had been brought to light.

DATA FILE

 BORN: November 2, 1865, Corsica (now Blooming Grove), Ohio
DIED: August 2, 1923

 INAUGURATED AS PRESIDENT: March 4, 1921, age 55

 KEY DATES:

1914   Elected as a senator for Ohio.

1921   Signs the Budget and Accounting Act, which creates the Bureau of the Budget.

1921   Signs peace agreements with Germany, Austria, and Hungary, made necessary by the failure of the United States to ratify the Treaty of Versailles.

Harding was an **avid musician** and **played** the **alto horn** in a **brass band**.

THE WASHINGTON NAVAL CONFERENCE

After World War I, there were concerns that a buildup of naval power might lead to a new war. In 1921, Harding helped set up a conference in Washington, D.C., to set limits on how many new warships could be built. Attended by nine nations, it was the first international conference held in the United States and resulted in a number of international agreements.

Warren G. Harding

CALVIN COOLIDGE

30th ★ 1923–1929   *Republican*

The son of a shopkeeper, Calvin Coolidge won public acclaim as governor of Massachusetts by boldly putting down a police strike in Boston. He became president after the sudden death of Harding in 1923, and restored faith in the office after the corruption scandals of the previous administration. A believer in minimal government interference, Coolidge governed with a light touch, vetoing many bills that he felt were too intrusive. He also kept the federal budget in the black and cut income taxes, but failed to spot the economic warning signs that led to the stock market crash of 1929.

THE GREAT MISSISSIPPI FLOOD

The flooding of the Mississippi River in April 1926 was among the worst in US history. Coolidge was criticized for his slow response and for trying to block federal spending that could help the flood victims. More than 250 people died and thousands were left homeless.

DATA FILE

BORN: July 4, 1872, Plymouth Notch, Vermont
DIED: January 5, 1933

INAUGURATED AS PRESIDENT: August 3, 1923, age 51

KEY DATES:

1924 Signs an Immigration Act into law, which cuts the number of migrants allowed to enter the United States. The act was designed to keep "undesirable" people out, specifically those of Asian ethnicities.

1926 Signs the Revenue Act into law, which reduces income taxes.

1928 Signs the Kellogg-Briand pact along with 14 other nations, agreeing not to settle international disputes through warfare.

Coolidge was **a man of few words,** which led to him being **nicknamed "Silent Cal."**

Calvin Coolidge

HERBERT HOOVER

31st ★ 1929–1933   *Republican*

Born into a Quaker family, Herbert Hoover made his fortune as a mining engineer. Before entering politics, he successfully organized a series of humanitarian efforts to provide food relief—achievements that made him a promising choice as president. However, just seven months after his inauguration, the stock market crashed. This led to the Great Depression, which blighted his presidency. Unemployment and poverty rose, and the measures Hoover took, such as lowering income tax, brought little relief.

DATA FILE

BORN: August 10, 1874, West Branch, Iowa
DIED: October 20, 1964

INAUGURATED AS PRESIDENT:
March 4, 1929, age 54

KEY DATES:

1917   Heads the US Food Administration to help America through shortages of food imports during World War I.

1930   Raises tariffs to protect American farmers from foreign imports, but this sets off a trade war and makes the Depression worse.

☞   Lou Hoover **p.133**

THE WALL STREET CRASH

On October 29, 1929, the US stock market (on Wall Street, New York City) crashed, triggering a nationwide economic panic. Businesses failed, unemployment soared, and banks went bankrupt. Hoover did not believe it was the government's job to provide assistance for people, so many relied on soup kitchens, such as the one shown below.

WITH THE FIRST LADY
President Hoover is pictured here with his wife, Lou Hoover. He first met her at Stanford University, California, where she was the only female geology major.

Hoover was so **unpopular** during the **Depression** that **town slums** were nicknamed **"Hoovervilles."**

Herbert Hoover

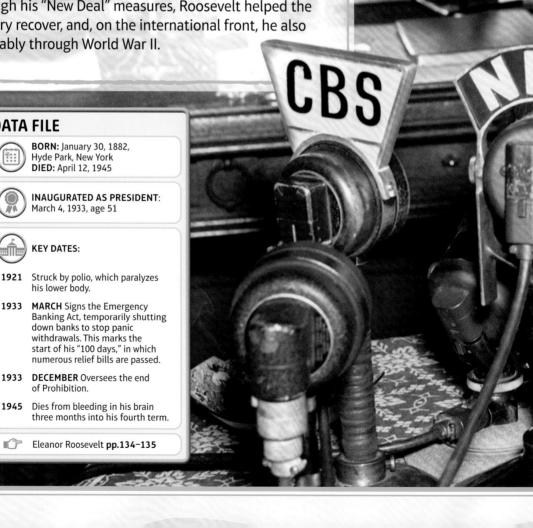

FRANKLIN D. ROOSEVELT

32nd ★ 1933–1945   *Democrat*

The longest-serving American president, Franklin D. Roosevelt won four terms in office and is remembered as one of the country's greatest leaders. Although he contracted polio in 1921, Roosevelt recovered and later became the governor of New York. He assumed the presidency during the Great Depression and introduced a range of programs to tackle the crisis, announcing to the nation "the only thing we have to fear is fear itself." Through his "New Deal" measures, Roosevelt helped the country recover, and, on the international front, he also led it ably through World War II.

DATA FILE

 BORN: January 30, 1882, Hyde Park, New York
DIED: April 12, 1945

 INAUGURATED AS PRESIDENT: March 4, 1933, age 51

 KEY DATES:

1921 Struck by polio, which paralyzes his lower body.

1933 **MARCH** Signs the Emergency Banking Act, temporarily shutting down banks to stop panic withdrawals. This marks the start of his "100 days," in which numerous relief bills are passed.

1933 **DECEMBER** Oversees the end of Prohibition.

1945 Dies from bleeding in his brain three months into his fourth term.

👉 Eleanor Roosevelt **pp.134–135**

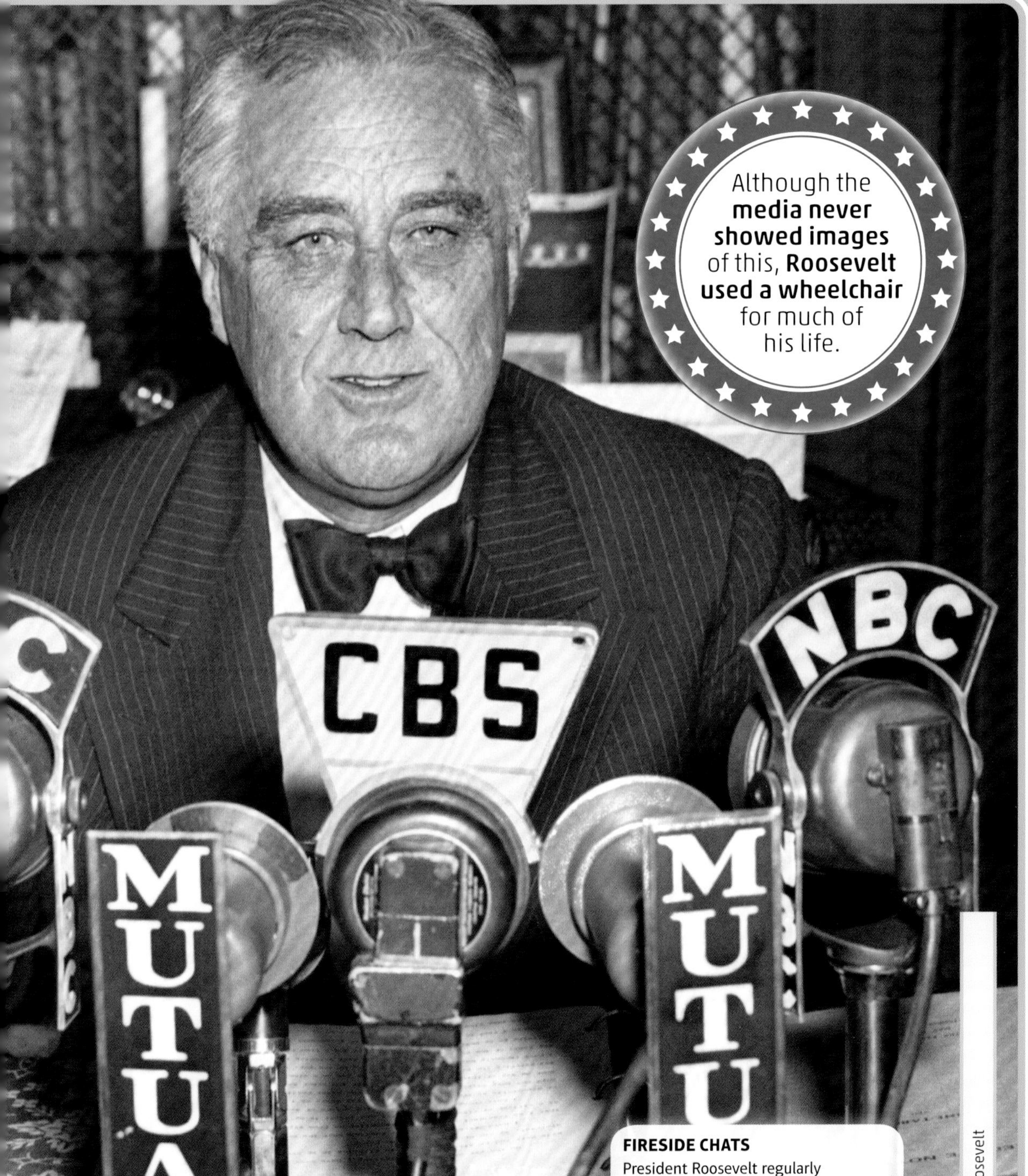
CBS
NBC
MUTUAL
MUTU

Although the **media never showed images** of this, **Roosevelt used a wheelchair** for much of his life.

FIRESIDE CHATS
President Roosevelt regularly addressed American citizens through radio broadcasts. Known as "fireside chats," these speeches reassured people during the Depression.

Franklin D. Roosevelt

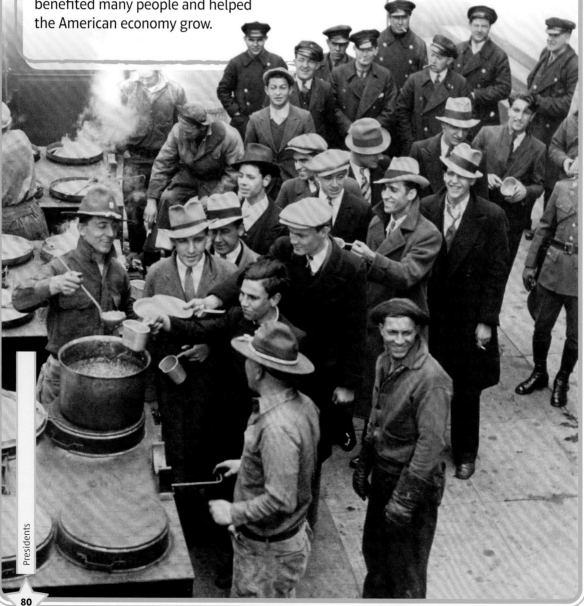

THE NEW DEAL

The Great Depression left 15 million people unemployed, something Roosevelt promised to address with a "New Deal" for Americans. As well as providing direct grants to the states so they could support their unemployed citizens, he set up a variety of federal programs to create jobs, including projects to build roads and plant trees. These initiatives benefited many people and helped the American economy grow.

RELIEF PROGRAMS
Roosevelt's work programs helped feed thousands of Americans. In this image, workers on a New Deal project in New York City receive a free meal.

PEARL HARBOR

Roosevelt's pledge to keep the United States out of World War II ended on December 7, 1941, when the Japanese launched a surprise bombing attack on the US naval base at Pearl Harbor. President Roosevelt called it "a date which will live in infamy" and declared war on Japan and its allies the next day. Over the next few years, Roosevelt gradually committed more troops to the war, leading to an eventual victory.

The **Japanese attack** at Pearl Harbor **lasted 110 minutes**.

HEAVY CASUALTIES

Smoke rises up from the *USS Arizona* after it was struck by Japanese bomber planes. In total, 2,400 American servicemen were killed and 19 ships destroyed in the Pearl Harbor attack.

Franklin D. Roosevelt

HARRY S. TRUMAN

33rd ★ 1945–1953   *Democrat*

A former haberdasher from Missouri, Harry S. Truman became president after Franklin D. Roosevelt's sudden death in 1945. As he led America through the last months of World War II, he faced huge challenges and ultimately approved the dropping of nuclear bombs on Japan. Truman's presidency marked the beginning of the Cold War between the United States and the communist Soviet Union, which saw tensions grow between the two countries. Truman took several actions to prevent the spread of Soviet communism to more countries. This "policy of containment" was known as the Truman Doctrine.

THE ATOMIC BOMB

After the US created an atomic bomb in May 1945, Truman and his administration decided to use this to end the war with Japan. In August that year, nuclear bombs were dropped on the Japanese cities of Hiroshima and Nagasaki. These caused a devastating impact and around 200,000 people died. Soon after, Japan surrendered.

DATA FILE

BORN: May 8, 1884, Lamar, Missouri
DIED: December 26, 1972

INAUGURATED AS PRESIDENT:
April 12, 1945, age 60

KEY DATES:

1947 Signs the National Security Act, which creates the CIA.

1948 Authorizes the Marshall Plan, which delivers billions of dollars to help Europe after World War II.

1948 Authorizes the Berlin Airlift, which delivers vital supplies to the city and stops it from becoming part of Soviet-controlled East Germany.

1950 Sends American troops to fight North Korean communists in the Korean War.

1950 Condemns a speech made by Senator Joseph McCarthy that accuses leading government officials of being communists. However, McCarthy's concerns lead to years of "McCarthyism," resulting in the persecution of many people suspected of being communists.

" Being the **President** is like **riding a tiger**. "

Harry S. Truman

DWIGHT D. EISENHOWER

34th ★ 1953–1961 *Republican*

A military hero, Dwight D. Eisenhower was the Supreme Commander of Allied Forces in Europe during World War II. Although he had no political experience, he won an easy victory when he ran for the presidency, promising to pursue a strong foreign policy. Once in office, Eisenhower struggled to contain communist expansion in Asia and the Middle East, while avoiding open war. Under his Eisenhower Doctrine, countries could request economic assistance or military aid from the US to combat communism. Even though he suffered from health problems during his second term, the country's strong economic growth ensured his good reputation.

Nicknamed Ike, Eisenhower used the **successful campaign slogan "I like Ike"** to get elected.

DATA FILE

BORN: October 14, 1890, Denison, Texas
DIED: March 28, 1969

INAUGURATED AS PRESIDENT:
January 20, 1953, age 62

KEY DATES:

1944   Leads the Allied forces that land in France on D-Day during World War II.

1945   Appointed Chief of Staff of the US Army.

1955   Attends the Geneva Conference with the leaders of Britain, France, and the Soviet Union.

Dwight D. Eisenhower

CIVIL RIGHTS

Due to continued racism, education in many Southern states was segregated well into the 1950s, with Black children made to attend separate schools from whites. In 1954, the Supreme Court declared this unconstitutional and ordered schools to desegregate immediately. However, when the school board in Little Rock, Arkansas, announced these plans, the Arkansas governor called in the National Guard to prevent Black students from entering the high school. Eisenhower was forced to send federal troops to ensure them safe access.

HOSTILE RECEPTION
Elizabeth Eckford was one of the nine Black students to attempt to enter the Central High School in Little Rock, Arkansas, on September 4, 1957. Pictured here, she faces angry crowds trying to block her entry.

The **first** **"astronaut"** of Project Mercury was a **rhesus monkey** called **Sam**.

THE SPACE RACE

In October 1957, the United States was surprised to hear the Soviet Union announce the launch of Sputnik 1, the first satellite, into space, starting a "space race" between the two superpowers. On January 31, 1958, the first US satellite, Explorer I, was launched. Later that year, Eisenhower created the National Aeronautics and Space Administration (NASA), with the task of sending an American astronaut into space.

PROJECT MERCURY

Launched in 1958, Project Mercury aimed to send an American into space before the Soviet Union made its own manned space flight. In 1961, Soviet astronaut Yuri Gagarin became the first man in space, followed just three weeks later by the first American, Alan Shepard (pictured top left).

Dwight D. Eisenhower

87

JOHN F. KENNEDY

35th ★ 1961–1963 *Democrat*

A charismatic leader whose speeches are still widely quoted today, John F. Kennedy was the youngest president ever elected. During his presidency, he pursued an active foreign policy, authorizing the use of military force to try to stop the spread of communism in Cuba and Vietnam. As Cold War tensions grew, he green-lit what became known as the Bay of Pigs invasion, a failed coup attempt in Cuba. He also convinced the Soviet Union to sign the Nuclear Test Ban Treaty, which limited the testing of nuclear weapons. At home, he promoted civil rights, sending what would become the Civil Rights Act of 1964 to Congress, and ordering troops to universities in the South to stop the racial segregation of students. Along with his wife Jackie, he revitalized the image of the US as a culturally sophisticated nation that valued the arts.

PRESIDENTIAL CAMPAIGN

As an attractive young couple, Kennedy and his wife Jackie appealed to many voters. Here they wave to crowds during a ticker-tape parade through New York City.

DATA FILE

BORN: May 29, 1917, Brookline, Massachusetts
DIED: November 22, 1963

INAUGURATED AS PRESIDENT: January 20, 1961, age 43

KEY DATES:

1961   **MARCH** Establishes the Peace Corps, a volunteer program for US citizens to provide aid to underdeveloped countries.

1961   **APRIL** Bay of Pigs debacle. After the failure of the invasion, Kennedy has to negotiate to get the prisoners released.

1961   **MAY** Announces to Congress his goal to put a man on the moon.

1963   **JUNE** Delivers a famous speech on civil rights, proposing a bill that was later passed by his successor, Lyndon B. Johnson.

1963   **JULY** Signs the Nuclear Test Ban Treaty with the Soviet Union.

1963   **NOVEMBER** Killed by an assassin at just 46 years old.

☞ Jacqueline Kennedy **p.136**

" Ask not what **your country can do** for you—ask **what you can do** for your country. "
John F. Kennedy, Inaugural Address, 1961

John F. Kennedy

89

NUCLEAR THREAT
Taken by American spy planes, aerial photographs such as this one showed the presence of missile equipment in Cuba, and would have been among the evidence presented to Kennedy.

THE CUBAN MISSILE CRISIS
In October 1962, US intelligence agencies found evidence that the Soviet Union was building nuclear missile bases in nearby Cuba. Since this severely threatened the security of the United States, Kennedy demanded that the bases be demolished and any missiles withdrawn. He then ordered a naval blockade of Cuba to stop Soviet ships from going to the island. As the US and the Soviet Union confronted each other, the world came close to a nuclear war. After a 13-day standoff, Soviet leader Nikita Khrushchev agreed to remove missiles from Cuba in exchange for Kennedy quietly withdrawing missiles from Turkey.

During the crisis, **officials pretended Kennedy had a cold** to explain why he did not appear in public.

ASSASSINATION

On November 22, 1963, Kennedy traveled to Dallas, Texas, to campaign for the 1964 elections. As the president rode through the city, an assassin opened fire, killing Kennedy almost immediately. This brutal murder of the young president was a tragedy that shocked the world. Lee Harvey Oswald was arrested for the murder, but he himself was shot dead two days later by Jack Ruby, a local nightclub owner. Oswald's reasons for assassinating Kennedy have remained unclear, and many people claim the assassination was part of a wider conspiracy.

A FATAL RIDE
When he was killed, Kennedy was traveling in an open limousine with his wife, Jackie. They were accompanied by Texas governor John Connally, who was also wounded in the shooting.

John F. Kennedy

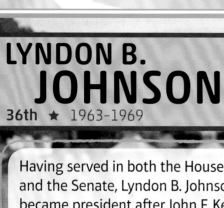

LYNDON B. JOHNSON

36th ★ 1963–1969   *Democrat*

Having served in both the House of Representatives and the Senate, Lyndon B. Johnson unexpectedly became president after John F. Kennedy's assassination. His dream was to build a "Great Society" through education and welfare reforms. As well as passing legislation to tackle poverty, Johnson promoted measures to end racial discrimination in employment and to ensure voting rights for Black people. Johnson's term is considered the height of the modern liberal movement since Roosevelt's New Deal. However, US involvement in Vietnam increased during his presidency, which made him unpopular.

ELECTION CAMPAIGN

Johnson is shown here addressing a campaign rally during the 1964 presidential election. He won by a wide margin, defeating his opponent Barry Goldwater.

DATA FILE

BORN: August 27, 1908, Stonewall, Texas
DIED: January 22, 1973

INAUGURATED AS PRESIDENT: November 22, 1963, age 55

KEY DATES:

1964 Signs the Civil Rights Act.

1964 Signs the Economic Opportunity Act, beginning his "war on poverty."

1965 Signs the Immigration and Nationality Act of 1965, which reformed US immigration policy and encouraged immigration from regions outside of Europe.

1965 **JULY 28** Authorizes sending American troops to Vietnam. The numbers increase rapidly to 400,000 by the end of 1966.

1965 **JULY 30** Signs Medicaid and Medicare into law, which provide hospital and medical insurance for poor and elderly Americans.

☞ "Lady Bird" Johnson **p.137**

Johnson was the **first** to take the **presidential oath** on board a **plane**.

Lyndon B. Johnson

THE CIVIL RIGHTS ACT

Although slavery had been abolished and Black people had been given voting rights, racism and discrimination remained deep-rooted nationwide, especially in the South. To help address this, in 1964 Johnson signed the Civil Rights Act, which outlawed segregation in hotels, restaurants, and other public places. It also made it illegal for employers to discriminate on the grounds of race. Johnson later followed this with the Voting Rights Act in 1965, which banned a range of practices, such as literacy tests, which had been used to prevent Black people from voting. He also passed the Fair Housing Act of 1968 which made discrimination in the sale or rental of housing illegal.

SIGNING THE ACT

Johnson helped pass numerous pieces of legislation to fulfill his vision of making the US a "Great Society." Here, the president shakes hands with the civil rights activist Dr. Martin Luther King, Jr., at the official signing of the Civil Rights Act.

THE VIETNAM WAR

Conflict in Vietnam had been ongoing since 1954, as the South Vietnamese government tried to fight off the communist forces of the Vietcong, who were supported by North Vietnam. The US had previously sent military advisors, but in 1964, after Congress passed the Gulf of Tonkin Resolution, Johnson made the decision to also send armed troops, and to bomb Vietcong bases in North Vietnam and Cambodia. The numbers of US soldiers grew steadily, from 3,500 in 1964 to 550,000 in 1968. As American casualties mounted, people from all walks of life took to the streets in huge antiwar demonstrations and, in March 1968, Johnson agreed to reduce the US presence in Vietnam.

TRANSPORTING TROOPS
Helicopters played an important role in transporting US troops to combat zones in Vietnam. The US forces were unused to the difficult terrain and suffered heavy losses during the fighting.

Lyndon B. Johnson

RICHARD M. NIXON

37th ★ 1969–1974   *Republican*

A sharp and determined political operator, Richard M. Nixon had served as Dwight D. Eisenhower's vice president before being elected to the presidency in 1968. Foreign policy dominated the first part of his presidency; he reduced the number of American troops in Vietnam and negotiated an end to the war, as well as signing an important arms control agreement with the Soviet Union. Nixon was also the first US president to visit China. At home, he took measures to control inflation, but his career was destroyed by the Watergate surveillance scandal and ended in his resignation.

Nixon is the **only president** to have **resigned**.

DATA FILE

BORN: January 9, 1913,
Yorba Linda, California
DIED: April 22, 1994

INAUGURATED AS PRESIDENT:
January 20, 1969, age 56

KEY DATES:

1970 Establishes the Environmental
Protection Agency to monitor
and control pollution.

1971 Coins the term "War on Drugs"
after he declared drug abuse to
be "public enemy number one."

1972 **FEBRUARY** Visits China to
establish diplomatic relations
between the two countries.

1972 **MAY** Signs the SALT agreement
with the Soviet Union, which
limits the number of nuclear
missiles each country is allowed
to possess.

Richard M. Nixon

" For **every American**, this has to be the **proudest day of their lives**. "
Nixon describing the moon landing

THE FIRST MAN ON THE MOON
In 1961, President Kennedy had announced the goal of landing a person on the moon within a decade, with the National Aeronautics and Space Administration (NASA) setting up the Apollo program to achieve this. On July 20, 1969, the Apollo 11 mission reached the moon and astronaut Neil Armstrong became the first man to set foot on its surface. The historic event was televised and Nixon spoke to the astronauts via a radio link to congratulate them.

Presidents

THE WATERGATE SCANDAL

In 1972, during Nixon's reelection campaign, several men broke into the Democratic National Committee's headquarters at the Watergate Hotel. Investigations into the burglary revealed that senior Republicans had tried to secretly record the Democrat campaign and had engaged in other illegal acts against their opponents. Nixon denied responsibility, but an audio recording system in Nixon's White House office revealed a cover-up. When the Senate threatened to impeach him in July 1974, Nixon resigned.

IMPEACH NIXON
Demonstrators call for the impeachment of Nixon in October 1973. If the president had not resigned, he would have faced a trial by the Senate and almost certain dismissal.

Richard M. Nixon

GERALD R. FORD

38th ★ 1974–1977 *Republican*

Gerald R. Ford rose to the office of president after Richard M. Nixon resigned over the Watergate scandal. A football star and law school graduate, Ford had earned a reputation for integrity during his many years of service in Congress. However, he soon lost his popularity after granting a "full, free, and absolute pardon" to Nixon. During his short term in office, he struggled to solve America's twin economic problems of rising inflation and unemployment. Overseas, Ford presided over the final stages of America's withdrawal from Vietnam. He also signed the Helsinki Accords to ease strained relations between the Soviet Union, the US, and other European countries.

DATA FILE

BORN: July 14, 1913, Omaha, Nebraska
DIED: December 26, 2006

INAUGURATED AS PRESIDENT:
August 9, 1974, age 61

KEY DATES:

1973 Becomes vice president after Spiro T. Agnew resigns over accusations of income tax fraud.

1974 Pardons former president Nixon.

1974 Forms the Economic Policy Board to provide advice to the president on financial issues.

1975 Escapes two assassination attempts.

 Betty Ford **p.138**

Ford is the **only president** who was **never elected** to the office of **president or vice president**.

THE FALL OF SAIGON

By 1975, the Vietcong Communist army had captured most of South Vietnam and were preparing to invade the city of Saigon. Many South Vietnamese troops fled by boat, but President Ford also ordered a massive airlift operation to rescue Americans and other civilians. This event marked the end of the Vietnam War.

Gerald R. Ford

JIMMY CARTER

39th ★ **1977-1981** *Democrat*

A native Georgian, Carter grew up on a peanut farm owned by his father. He took office at a difficult time and despite promoting many social reforms, rising unemployment and inflation dented his reputation. Abroad, Carter pursued a compassionate foreign policy, pushing for human rights and negotiating peace treaties. However, his presidency also saw the renewal of Cold War tensions with the Soviet Union after the Soviet army invaded Afghanistan in 1979. The end of his term was overshadowed by the Iran hostage crisis, when militant students in Tehran held American diplomats hostage for over a year and Carter struggled to gain their release.

THE CAMP DAVID ACCORDS

In September 1978, Carter invited Egyptian President Anwar Sadat (left) and Israeli Prime Minister Menachem Begin (right) to the presidential retreat at Camp David. They signed a historic agreement 13 days later, bringing about peace between their two countries for the first time since 1947.

DATA FILE

BORN: October 1, 1924, Plains, Georgia

INAUGURATED AS PRESIDENT: January 20, 1977, age 52

KEY DATES:

1977 Signs the Panama Canal Treaty, agreeing to return control of the canal and surrounding land to Panama.

1978 Attempts to tackle the energy crisis by removing controls on domestic oil and gas prices, leading to a large increase in prices for American consumers.

1979 Signs the SALT II agreement on arms control with the Soviet Union, but withdraws from it after the Soviet Union invades Afghanistan.

2002 Awarded the Nobel Peace Prize for his role in helping resolve international conflicts, and in particular the Camp David Accords.

Rosalynn Carter **p.139**

Before entering politics, Carter **served in the navy** as a **submariner**.

Jimmy Carter

RONALD REAGAN

40th ★ 1981-1989 *Republican*

Known as the "Great Communicator," Ronald Reagan began his career as a movie actor before going on to serve eight years as the governor of California. He survived an assassination attempt early in his presidency, and then spent most of his first term implementing "Reaganomics"—a program of reducing taxes and cutting back on welfare programs. His policies cut inflation but when the economy went into a downturn, government debt increased to more than $2 trillion. Despite this setback, Reagan remained an extremely popular president who heavily influenced modern Republican ideals. His Reagan Doctrine of reversing communism helped to end the Cold War.

DATA FILE

 BORN: February 6, 1911, Tampico, Illinois
DIED: June 5, 2004

 INAUGURATED AS PRESIDENT: January 20, 1981, age 69

 KEY DATES:

1981 Appoints the first female justice, Sandra Day O'Connor, to the Supreme Court.

1984 Reelected for a second term, with the second-largest victory margin in the 20th century.

1986 Passes the Anti-Drug Abuse Act through Congress, authorizing $1.7 trillion to fund the War on Drugs along with mandatory sentences for drug-related offenses.

 Nancy Reagan p.140

Reagan was an **anticommunist informer** for the **FBI** in Hollywood in the **1940s**.

Ronald Reagan

THE LEADERS MEET
Pictured here in November 1985, Reagan and Mikhail Gorbachev meet during the American-Soviet summit in Geneva. These meetings began to ease longstanding tensions between the two countries.

SUMMITS WITH GORBACHEV

Relations with the Soviet Union were strained in the early years of Reagan's presidency, with Reagan calling it an "evil empire." He ordered the creation of the Strategic Defense Initiative ("Star Wars"), a project to shoot down Soviet missiles if they attacked the US. However, when Mikhail Gorbachev, the new Soviet leader, promised reform in 1985, Reagan reached out to him. They signed a treaty in 1987, agreeing to limit their nuclear weapons.

THE IRAN-CONTRA AFFAIR

In 1986, it was revealed that members of Reagan's government were secretly selling weapons to Iran via Israel to gain the release of American hostages in Lebanon. This caused a scandal, as Reagan had publicly opposed selling arms to Iran. Additionally, the profit from these sales was being sent to the Contras—opponents of the communist regime in Nicaragua—support for whom was banned by Congress. Investigations took place but the extent of Reagan's involvement remained unclear.

CONGRESSIONAL HEARINGS

A congressional committee held televised hearings to get to the bottom of the scandal. Here, Lieutenant Colonel Oliver North, one of several key figures involved in the affair, testifies before the committee.

Ronald Reagan

GEORGE H. W.
BUSH

41st ★ 1989–1993   *Republican*

A former Texas oil man, George H. W. Bush was Ronald Reagan's vice president for eight years. His presidency was dominated by foreign affairs, including the challenges caused by the collapse of the Soviet Union, and the Gulf War, which broke out when Iraq invaded Kuwait. At home, he passed measures to cut government debt, but his support of tax increases and growing unemployment cost him reelection.

DATA FILE

 BORN: June 12, 1924, Milton, Massachusetts
DIED: November 30, 2018

 INAUGURATED AS PRESIDENT: January 20, 1989, age 64

 KEY DATES:

1989 Sends US forces into Panama to capture its president, who was suspected of involvement in drug trafficking.

1990 Signs the Americans with Disabilities Act, which makes it illegal for employers to discriminate based on disability.

1990 Sends US troops to expel Iraqi forces in Kuwait.

 Barbara Bush **p.141**

Bush became **hard of hearing** after **piloting** noisy **bomber aircraft** during **World War II**.

THE FALL OF THE BERLIN WALL

After World War II, Germany had been divided into communist East Germany (supported by the Soviet Union) and capitalist West Germany (supported by the US). In 1989, after demonstrations against its government, East Germany allowed people to cross the Berlin Wall, which had formerly prevented free movement between the two sides of the country. This symbolic event marked the end of the Cold War, and led to the eventual reunification of Germany in October 1990, which President Bush helped negotiate.

THE WALL COMES DOWN

On November 9, 1989, an announcement that East Germans could travel freely to the West led to thousands crossing the Berlin Wall, which divided the two halves of the city. Many took to knocking down parts of the wall themselves, while others celebrated by climbing on top of the wall.

George H. W. Bush

BILL CLINTON

42nd ★ 1993-2001   *Democrat*

The youthful image of William J. Clinton (known as Bill) and his promises to reform health care and balance the budget meant his presidency began with a sense of hope. During his first term, he achieved much abroad with his involvement in peace deals in Northern Ireland, Bosnia, and the Middle East, and at home he presided over the longest period of US economic expansion during peacetime. However, when the Democrats lost control of both houses of Congress, his health care reforms were watered down. He signed the North American Free Trade Agreement (NAFTA) into law after it was ratified by Congress. Although he remained popular, the end of his presidency was overshadowed by personal scandals.

In **high school**, Clinton **played** in a **jazz band** called **Three Blind Mice**.

WINNING TWO TERMS
Clinton was reelected in the 1996 presidential race, even though the Republicans had gained control of Congress in 1994. He was the first Democrat to win two terms since Franklin D. Roosevelt.

DATA FILE

BORN: August 19, 1946, Hope, Arkansas

INAUGURATED AS PRESIDENT: January 20, 1993, age 46

KEY DATES:

1978 Elected governor of Arkansas.

1994 Introduces a crime bill, which is held is held to be responsible for mass incarceration, especially of Black people.

1995 Clashes with the Republican-led Congress on the best way to balance the budget. This leads to a temporary government shutdown.

1995 Visits Northern Ireland, where he plays a key role in bringing about the historic Good Friday agreement, which ended 30 years of conflict between different political groups.

1998 Impeachment proceedings brought against him for having lied under oath about an affair with a White House intern. He is later acquitted.

☞ Hillary Clinton **p.142**

THE WYE RIVER SUMMIT

Longstanding conflict between Arabs and Jewish settlers in Palestine worsened after the establishment of Israel in 1947. In 1998, Clinton invited Israeli Prime Minister Benjamin Netanyahu and Palestinian leader Yasser Arafat for peace talks near Wye Mills, Maryland. Although he secured an agreement, fighting has yet to cease.

Bill Clinton

GEORGE W. BUSH

43rd ★ 2001–2009   *Republican*

The son of a former president, George W. Bush worked in the family oil business before entering politics. He won the 2000 presidential race by a very narrow margin—losing the popular vote but winning the Electoral College—but went on to serve two full terms in office. Bush's presidency was largely defined by the 9/11 terrorist attacks. In their aftermath, he called for Americans to understand that "Islam is peace." He went on to declare a "War on Terror." As part of this, he sent US troops to Afghanistan to dismantle the terrorist organization al-Qaeda, and to Iraq to overthrow the dictator Saddam Hussein.

Bush escaped an **assassination attempt** in 2005 when a live **grenade** thrown at him **failed to explode**.

DATA FILE

BORN: July 6, 1946, New Haven, Connecticut

INAUGURATED AS PRESIDENT: January 20, 2001, age 54

KEY DATES:

2001 **MARCH** Withdraws support from the Kyoto Protocol, which commits participating countries to reducing their greenhouse gas emissions in order to help prevent global warming.

2001 **MAY** Signs a law approving a $1.35 trillion package of tax cuts. As a result, the government debt increases.

2001 **OCTOBER** Signs the controversial Patriot Act, which gives increased powers to government agencies to carry out surveillance.

2001 **OCTOBER** Launches military action in Afghanistan.

2002 Signs into law the No Child Left Behind Act, which introduces new testing measures and makes schools more accountable for the progress of their students.

☞ Laura Bush **p.143**

☞ Extraordinary Elections **pp.196–197**

BUSH AND THE MARINES
President Bush speaks to US Marines at Camp Pendleton on December 7, 2004—the 63rd anniversary of the Japanese attack on Pearl Harbor. During his time in office, Bush significantly increased spending on defense.

George W. Bush

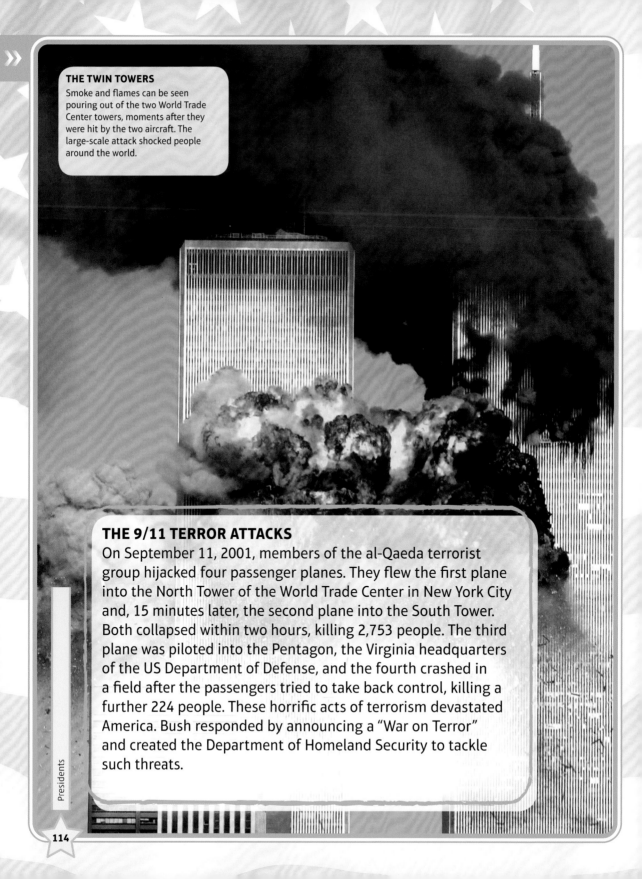

THE TWIN TOWERS
Smoke and flames can be seen pouring out of the two World Trade Center towers, moments after they were hit by the two aircraft. The large-scale attack shocked people around the world.

THE 9/11 TERROR ATTACKS

On September 11, 2001, members of the al-Qaeda terrorist group hijacked four passenger planes. They flew the first plane into the North Tower of the World Trade Center in New York City and, 15 minutes later, the second plane into the South Tower. Both collapsed within two hours, killing 2,753 people. The third plane was piloted into the Pentagon, the Virginia headquarters of the US Department of Defense, and the fourth crashed in a field after the passengers tried to take back control, killing a further 224 people. These horrific acts of terrorism devastated America. Bush responded by announcing a "War on Terror" and created the Department of Homeland Security to tackle such threats.

THE IRAQ WAR

In 2002, Bush accused the Iraqi government—led by Saddam Hussein—of developing chemical and nuclear weapons. Although United Nations inspectors found no evidence of these weapons, the US, and a coalition of allies, invaded Iraq in 2003. US troops took control of the capital, Baghdad, on April 9, and removed Hussein's government. The ensuing power vacuum led to insurrection, civil war, and the eventual emergence of ISIS. By 2016, more than 4,800 American soldiers and an estimated half a million Iraqi people had died.

PREPARING TO INVADE
US armored forces move into position on the Kuwait-Iraq border, two days ahead of the invasion of Iraq in March 2003.

BARACK
OBAMA

44th ★ 2009–2017   *Democrat*

A constitutional law professor and Illinois senator, Barack Obama was the first Black person to be elected president. In his first term, he passed measures to reduce the impact of the global economic crisis of 2008, to introduce affordable federally funded health care, and to withdraw American troops from Afghanistan and Iraq. Obama continued to be active abroad during his second term and made a deal with Iran to limit its nuclear activities. Due to the continuing threat of global terrorism, he sent US forces to help stop the spread of the terrorist organization Islamic State in Iraq and Syria.

CONFIDENT STATESMAN

A charismatic leader, President Obama is pictured here greeting schoolchildren assembled on the South Lawn of the White House. In the 2008 election, he promoted a message of hope and change, inspiring many to vote for him.

Obama has **won two Grammy Awards**, for spoken word **narrations of his books**.

DATA FILE

BORN: August 4, 1961, Honolulu, Hawaii

INAUGURATED AS PRESIDENT: January 20, 2009, age 47

KEY DATES:

2009 Signs the American Recovery and Reinvestment Act, to help the US economy recover from the global economic crisis.

2011 **MAY** Informs the nation that a team of US Navy Seals has killed the terrorist leader Osama bin Laden in Abbottabad, Pakistan.

2011 **DECEMBER** Finishes withdrawing American troops from Iraq.

2014 Orders airstrikes against Islamic State positions in Iraq.

2015 **JUNE** Supreme Court declares same-sex marriage legal in all 50 states.

☞ Michelle Obama pp.144–145

Barack Obama

THE AFFORDABLE CARE ACT

Past attempts to provide federal funding for health care had always failed or been vetoed. After a 2000 World Health Organization report placed the US 37th in global health care rankings, Obama put forth measures to improve this, which became known as "Obamacare." These became law in March 2010, and made individual health insurance compulsory for those not covered by their employers, as well as creating federal subsidies for health insurance for the poor.

DOCTORS FOR OBAMA
Supporters of Obama's Affordable Care Act, known as ACA or Obamacare, rally outside the Supreme Court in June 2015. The court ruled against a claim that some elements of the act were unconstitutional.

IMPROVED RELATIONS WITH CUBA

Relations between the US and Cuba had been strained since 1959. After Fidel Castro's communist government came to power, the US had broken off diplomatic and business ties with Cuba. In 2015, Obama sought to remedy this situation. He removed Cuba from a list of countries that sponsor terrorism; made it easier for Americans to travel there; reopened the US embassy in Havana; and in 2016, became the first US president to visit the island since 1928.

HAND OF FRIENDSHIP
Obama greets Cuban president Raúl Castro at the United Nations in September 2015—a symbol of the thaw in Cuban-American relations after nearly 60 years of tension.

Barack Obama

DONALD TRUMP

45th ★ 2017–2021   *Republican*

Businessman and reality television star Donald J. Trump's term was filled with controversies. Trump tried to make good on his campaign promise to curb immigration to America, including enacting a travel ban on citizens from Muslim-majority countries and building a wall between the US and Mexico. He also pulled the US out of the Paris Climate Agreement. Trump upended many norms in American politics, especially in his often-inflammatory use of Twitter, and called accurate journalism that he didn't like "fake news." In 2020, Trump was impeached by the House of Representatives, although the Republican-controlled Senate acquitted him.

Trump was the **first president** not to serve in the **government or military** before assuming **office**.

SUPREME COURT JUDGES

Trump appointed two conservative judges, Neil Gorsuch and Brett Kavanaugh, to the United States Supreme Court. A third, Amy Coney Barrett, was confirmed in October 2020, less than a month before the presidential elections. Nine judges serve on the Supreme Court for lifetime terms. Barrett replaces Justice Ruth Badger Ginsburg after her death in 2020, and changes the court's balance from a five-four to a six-three conservative-liberal split.

DATA FILE

BORN: June 14, 1946, New York, New York

INAUGURATED AS PRESIDENT: January 20, 2017, age 70

KEY DATES:

2018 **APRIL** The Trump administration begins separation of immigrant children from their families at the Mexican border.

2018 **MAY** Trump pulls the US out of the Iran nuclear deal.

2018 **JUNE** Trump holds a summit with North Korean leader Kim Jong-un.

2020 **OCTOBER** Trump announces he has tested positive for Covid-19.

Donald Trump

JOE BIDEN

46th ★ 2021 — *Democrat*

Taking office after the controversial and divisive Trump presidency, Joseph R. Biden, Jr. (known as Joe) won citizens over with his promise of an administration rooted in rebuilding American unity. Biden's service in government began as a senator from Delaware in 1972, a post he held until he was elected as Barack Obama's vice-president in 2004. He helped pass the Affordable Care Act in 2010, and became known as a vigorous supporter of LGBTQ+ rights. Having once supported tough on crime policies, he has talked recently of the need for reform and backed Black Lives Matter. His campaign platform in 2020 included support of a Green New Deal, a promise to implement a compassionate immigration policy, and a plan to fight the Covid-19 pandemic.

LIFELONG EXPERIENCE

In 1972, Joe Biden's first wife and baby daughter were killed in a car accident. The newly elected senator commuted between Washington, D.C., and Delaware to be with his two young sons every night. In 2015, Beau, the eldest, died of cancer. Biden's second wife, Jill (pictured with the boys and daughter Ashley), has talked of how tragedy over his long political career has made Joe a more resilient and empathic leader.

JOE
BIDEN
PRESIDENT

At the **age of** 78, Joe Biden became the **oldest person** to be elected president.

DATA FILE

BORN: November 20, 1942, Scranton, Pennsylvania

INAUGURATED AS PRESIDENT: January 20, 2021, age 78

KEY DATES:

1972 Elected to the US Senate from Delaware at the age of 30.

1994 Cosponsors the Violence Against Women Act with Republican Senator Orrin Hatch.

2008 Runs for the Democratic nomination for president against Barack Obama but loses. Obama asks him to be his vice president.

2017 Receives Presidential Medal of Freedom for his years of service to the country.

Joe Biden

2 NOTABLE FIRST LADIES

Since Martha Washington in the 18th century, the wives of the US presidents have held a highly visible yet undefined position. Their role has evolved over the centuries, from hosting functions and events in the White House, to using their influence to promote specific causes.

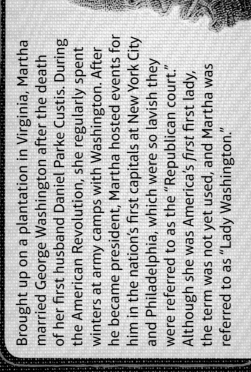

MARTHA
WASHINGTON

1789–1797

Brought up on a plantation in Virginia, Martha married George Washington after the death of her first husband Daniel Parke Custis. During the American Revolution, she regularly spent winters at army camps with Washington. After he became president, Martha hosted events for him in the nation's first capitals at New York City and Philadelphia, which were so lavish they were referred to as the "Republican court." Although she was America's *first* first lady, the term was not yet used, and Martha was referred to as "Lady Washington."

Martha is **one of only two women** to appear on **US paper currency**—the other is **Pocahontas.**

DATA FILE

BORN: June 2, 1731, New Kent County, Virginia
DIED: May 22, 1802

MARRIED: January 6, 1759, New Kent County, Virginia

CHILDREN: Daniel, Frances, John, Martha

KEY DATES:

1757   Becomes a widow after the death of her first husband.

1778   Spends the winter at Valley Forge, Pennsylvania, tending to sick soldiers in the Continental Army.

1797   Returns to live at Mount Vernon after the end of George Washington's presidency.

Martha Washington

ABIGAIL ADAMS
1797-1801

Although she had no formal education, Abigail was an avid reader. She championed the cause of educating girls and promoted the rights of married women. She also inspired future first ladies to play an active role in politics. After the American Revolution, Abigail accompanied John Adams on diplomatic postings to France and Great Britain. They were the first presidential couple to live in the White House.

DATA FILE

 BORN: November 22, 1744, Weymouth, Massachusetts
DIED: October 28, 1818

 MARRIED: October 25, 1764 Weymouth, Massachusetts

 CHILDREN: Abigail ("Nabby"), John Quincy, Susanna, Charles, Thomas Boylston

 KEY DATES:

1775 Serves on a commission in Massachusetts to test the loyalty of women suspected of working against the Revolution.

1789 Becomes the first second lady when her husband becomes Washington's vice president.

1800 Moves into the White House.

DOLLEY MADISON

1809–1817

A lively and charming hostess, Dolley began the tradition of inaugural balls in Washington, D.C. She was the first to decorate the White House, and in 1810, threw a gala to display the remodeled mansion. Dolley is also remembered for the remarkable courage she displayed when the British invaded Washington, D.C., during the War of 1812. As British troops advanced to burn the White House, she rescued several national treasures, including a large portrait of George Washington.

DATA FILE

 BORN: May 20, 1768, New Garden, North Carolina
DIED: July 12, 1849

 MARRIED: September 15, 1794 Harewood, Virginia

 CHILDREN: John Payne, William

 KEY DATES:

1809   Presides at the first inaugural ball in Washington, D.C.

1814   Saves valuables from the White House before it is burned.

1844   Becomes the first private citizen to broadcast a message via Morse Code.

MARY TODD
LINCOLN
1861–1865

Mary was a well-educated, intelligent, and witty woman, but led a troubled life under the pressures of her husband's political success and family tragedy. During the Civil War, she visited patients in the Union army hospitals and supported efforts to raise money to help freed slaves. However, jealous rivals accused her of being a Confederate sympathizer due to her Southern roots, and she was also criticized for spending large amounts of money on clothes. The grief she suffered after both the death of her son Willie and her husband's assassination made the last years of her life almost unbearable.

DATA FILE

 BORN: December 13, 1818, Lexington, Kentucky
DIED: July 16, 1882

 MARRIED: November 4, 1842, Springfield, Illinois

 CHILDREN: Robert Todd, Edward Baker, William Wallace, Thomas

 KEY DATES:

1861 Spends $26,000 restoring the White House, leading to accusations of extravagance.

1865 Witnesses the assassination of President Lincoln while at Ford's Theatre in Washington, D.C.

Notable First Ladies

FRANCES CLEVELAND

1885-1889/1893-1897

Frances became the *first* first lady to wed in the White House when she married Grover Cleveland, whom she had known since she was a child. The youngest first lady, she was a popular hostess who held receptions on Saturdays so that working women could attend. During her time in Washington, D.C., she championed several charities, including those that supported homeless women and families, and others that promoted education for girls.

DATA FILE

 BORN: July 21, 1864, Buffalo, New York
DIED: October 29, 1947

 MARRIED: June 2, 1886, White House, Washington, D.C.

 CHILDREN: Ruth, Esther, Marion, Richard Folsom, Francis Grover

 KEY DATES:

1887 Accompanies President Cleveland on a tour of the southern and western states.

1893 Becomes the first former first lady to return to the White House when Grover Cleveland is reelected for a nonconsecutive second term.

Mary Todd Lincoln/Frances Cleveland

EDITH
WILSON

1915–1921

As first lady during World War I, Edith set an example by volunteering with the Red Cross and encouraging rationing in the White House. After the president had a stroke in 1919, she took on a stewardship role, working with his cabinet and reading government papers. By doing this, she hid the poor state of the president's health, allowing him to continue in office.

DATA FILE

 BORN: October 15, 1872, Wytheville, Virginia
DIED: December 28, 1961

 MARRIED: December 1915, Washington, D.C.

 KEY DATES:

1896 Marries her first husband, businessman Norman Galt, who dies in 1908.

1915 First meets the president, shortly after the death of his first wife Ellen.

1919 Accompanies President Wilson to Europe to attend the peace negotiations at Versailles, at the end of World War I.

LOU HOOVER

1929-1933

Lou led an active life before becoming first lady. An expert horsewoman and trained geologist, she accompanied Herbert Hoover on his travels as a mining engineer, and later became involved with food relief charities during World War I. As first lady, she lobbied for women's rights and gave radio speeches encouraging Americans as the Great Depression deepened.

DATA FILE

 BORN: March 29, 1874, Waterloo, Iowa
DIED: January 7, 1944

 MARRIED: February 10, 1899, Monterey, California

 CHILDREN: Herbert Clark, Allan Henry

 KEY DATES:

1914 Creates and chairs the American Women's War Relief Fund.

1923 Appointed President of the Women's Division of the National Amateur Athletics Association.

When **accompanying** her **husband to China, Lou learned to speak Mandarin Chinese**.

Edith Wilson/Lou Hoover

ELEANOR
ROOSEVELT
1933–1945

Eleanor was one of the most active first ladies, and also the longest-serving. A great believer in social reform, she took President Franklin Roosevelt on a tour of New York slums early in their courtship. Once he became president, she campaigned on a wide range of social issues. A champion of women's rights, she ensured her husband's New Deal—a social reform program—contained measures to help them. She held press conferences at the White House for female reporters, wrote *My Day*—a daily newspaper column—and gave more than 1,400 speeches during her time as first lady.

Eleanor **helped draft** the **Universal Declaration of Human Rights**.

OFFICIAL VISITS

After she left high school, Eleanor worked for the National Consumers League, visiting slums and reporting on their conditions. As first lady, she continued to visit institutions across the country, including schools and other government facilities. Her findings encouraged her to promote many new causes.

DATA FILE

BORN: October 11, 1884,
New York, New York
DIED: November 7, 1962

MARRIED: March 17, 1905,
New York, New York

CHILDREN: Anna Eleanor;
James; Elliott; Franklin
Delano, Jr.; John Aspinwall

KEY DATES:

1939   **FEBRUARY** Resigns from the
Daughters of the American
Revolution (DAR) after they
refuse to allow a Black
singer to perform at
Constitution Hall.

1939   **JUNE** Hosts British monarchs King
George VI and Queen Elizabeth
when they visit the US.

1946   Leads the UN Commission on
Human Rights as chairwoman
for six years.

1961   Becomes Chair of the
Presidential Commission
on the Status of Women.

SPEAKING HER MIND

In this photograph, Eleanor
is shown speaking at the
annual *Herald Tribune* forum
in New York, 1943. Although
controversial at the time, her
outspokenness made her one
of history's most influential
first ladies.

Eleanor Roosevelt

JACQUELINE
KENNEDY
1961–1963

Jacqueline—popularly known as Jackie—brought a sense of style and flair to the office of first lady. A French literature graduate with an interest in the arts, she refurbished the White House and used it to stage opera, jazz, and ballet performances. Jackie accompanied her husband on many trips abroad, making more international tours than any previous first lady. A popular figure, her strength and quiet dignity after the tragic assassination of her husband won her the admiration of millions of people worldwide.

DATA FILE

 BORN: July 28, 1929, Southampton, New York
DIED: May 19, 1994

 MARRIED: September 12, 1953, Newport, Rhode Island

 CHILDREN: Caroline; Patrick; John Fitzgerald, Jr.

 KEY DATES:

1952   Gets her first job as a reporter for the *Washington Times-Herald*.

1962   Presents a televised tour of the White House.

"LADY BIRD" JOHNSON

1963–1969

Nicknamed "Lady Bird," Claudia Taylor was born into a well-to-do Texas family. After graduating from college, she bought a small radio station and built it up into a large media business. As first lady, Lady Bird championed civil rights and held "Women Do-er Luncheons" in the White House to promote the accomplishments of leading women in their respective fields. She also supported a program for the beautification of Washington, D.C., and helped refurbish decayed public buildings.

DATA FILE

 BORN: December 22, 1912, Karnack, Texas
DIED: July 11, 2007

 MARRIED: November 17, 1934, San Antonio, Texas

 CHILDREN: Lynda Bird, Luci Baines

 KEY DATES:

1965 Becomes honorary chairperson of the Head Start program, which aims to help educate preschool children in poor families.

1982 Founds the Lady Bird Johnson Wildflower Center at the University of Texas.

In **1970**, Lady Bird **published *A White House Diary*** about her experiences as first lady.

Jacqueline Kennedy/"Lady Bird" Johnson

BETTY **FORD**

1974–1977

Betty studied dance, and worked as a model and a department store fashion coordinator, before becoming first lady. She was a strong champion of women's rights and campaigned to introduce an Equal Rights Amendment to the Constitution. A frank and open first lady, her discussions about her breast cancer surgery inspired other women to talk about the difficult subject. After leaving the White House, she admitted to a long-running struggle with alcoholism.

DATA FILE

 BORN: April 8, 1918, Chicago, Illinois
DIED: July 8, 2011

 MARRIED: October 15, 1948, Grand Rapids, Michigan

 CHILDREN: Michael Gerald, John "Jack" Gardner, Steven Meigs, Susan Elizabeth

 KEY DATES:

1975 Becomes the first recipient of the National Woman's Party Alice Paul Award to honor her campaign for the Equal Rights Amendment.

1982 Founds the Betty Ford Center for alcohol and drug dependency, after her own battle with alcoholism.

In **1976**, Betty became the *first* first lady to appear in a **television sitcom**.

ROSALYNN
CARTER

1977–1981

A small-town girl, Rosalynn became an active first lady and was the first to attend cabinet meetings. She spoke out on improving mental health care, testifying before Congress on the issue. Rosalynn also pushed for the introduction of an Age Discrimination Act to help elderly Americans.

DATA FILE

 BORN: August 18, 1927, Plains, Georgia

 MARRIED: July 7, 1946, Plains, Georgia

 CHILDREN: John William, James Earl III, Donnel Jeffrey, Amy Lynn

 KEY DATES:

1980 Campaigns actively for the passing of the Mental Health Systems Act, which reforms mental health treatment.

1982 Presides as vice chairperson of the Carter Center, a nonprofit organization founded by her and her husband, which aims to promote health and human rights around the world.

Betty Ford/ Rosalynn Carter

NANCY
REAGAN
1981–1989

Like Ronald Reagan, Nancy was a former Hollywood actor. As first lady, she fought hard for better drug education, and started the "Just Say No" campaign across America. She also supported the Foster Grandparent Program to help children in difficult circumstances. Nancy was fiercely protective of her husband, especially after he suffered an assassination attempt.

DATA FILE

 BORN: July 6, 1921, New York, New York
DIED: March 6, 2016

 MARRIED: March 4, 1952, San Fernando Valley, California

 CHILDREN: Patricia Ann "Patti," Ronald Prescott

 KEY DATES:

1985 Holds a conference in Washington for the first ladies of 17 countries to highlight the problem of drug and alcohol abuse among children.

1988 Becomes the *first* first lady to address the United Nations, asking for tougher laws to prevent the illegal movement of drugs.

BARBARA
BUSH
1989–1993

Barbara and George H. W. Bush met as teenagers and married during World War II. As first lady, Barbara's warm nature and approachable air gave her a reputation as "America's grandmother." She was active in promoting adult literacy—an interest that stemmed from her son Neil's dyslexia—and organized the Barbara Bush Foundation for Family Literacy. She also supported numerous other causes, including those concerning the homeless and the elderly.

DATA FILE

 BORN: June 8, 1925, Rye, New York
DIED: April 17, 2018

 MARRIED: January 6, 1945, Rye, New York

 CHILDREN: George Walker, Robin, John Ellis "Jeb," Neil Mallon, Marvin Pierce, Dorothy Walker

 KEY DATES:

1989 Establishes the Barbara Bush Foundation for Family Literacy.

1994 Publishes her autobiography *Barbara Bush: A Memoir*.

HILLARY CLINTON
1993–2001

Born in Chicago, Hillary earned a law degree from Yale University. One of the most politically active first ladies, she was the first to have her own office in the West Wing. She pushed for health care reforms and supported measures to help adopted children. In 2000, Hillary became the first presidential spouse to be elected to political office, as a senator for New York state. She then served as Secretary of State for four years in President Obama's administration.

DATA FILE

BORN: October 26, 1947
Park Ridge, Illinois

MARRIED: October 11, 1975
Fayetteville, Arkansas

CHILDREN: Chelsea

KEY DATES:

1997 Sponsors the Adoption and Safe Family Act to provide extra funds for adopted children and their families.

2009 Appointed Secretary of State.

2016 Becomes the first female presidential nominee of a major political party (the Democrats), losing the election to Republican Donald Trump.

Notable First Ladies

LAURA
BUSH
2001–2009

A former schoolteacher, Laura had a strong interest in child literacy. She championed George W. Bush's No Child Left Behind Act to raise the standards of education, particularly in poor areas. Laura also promoted programs such as the New Teacher Project, which aimed to attract professionals from different career backgrounds into teaching. To promote reading at an early age, she created a national initiative called "Ready to Read, Ready to Learn."

DATA FILE

 BORN: November 4, 1946, Midland, Texas

 MARRIED: November 5, 1977, Midland, Texas

 CHILDREN: Barbara, Jenna

 KEY DATES:

2002   Establishes The Laura Bush Foundation for America's Libraries.

2004   Helps in the creation of the Preserve America History Teacher of the Year award, a part of her campaign to increase interest in the historical heritage of the United States.

In **2001**, Laura **launched** the **first annual National Book Festival** across the country.

Hillary Clinton/Laura Bush

MICHELLE
OBAMA
2009–2017

A Harvard Law School graduate, Michelle was Vice President of Community Affairs at the University of Chicago before becoming first lady. The first Black first lady, she became a role model for women around the world and championed the right of girls to receive a proper education. As part of a campaign to reduce child obesity, she planted a vegetable garden on the White House lawn to encourage healthy food habits. Michelle also raised awareness of the difficulties faced by military veterans' families, and helped improve access to higher education for poorer students.

Michelle's **Secret Service code name** was **"Renaissance."**

LET'S MOVE

In 2010, Michelle launched "Let's Move," a campaign to reduce childhood obesity levels in the United States, after statistics showed around 40 percent of children were overweight or obese. The campaign aimed to work with communities and educators to promote healthy eating and exercise among the young.

DATA FILE

BORN: January 17, 1964, Chicago, Illinois

MARRIED: October 3, 1992, Chicago, Illinois

CHILDREN: Malia Ann, Natasha "Sasha"

KEY DATES:

2011 Launches "Joining Forces," an initiative to raise awareness of the issues faced by veterans and their families.

2014 Founds "Reach Higher" with the aim of encouraging education beyond high school for children from poorer families.

2015 Launches the "Let Girls Learn" initiative to help girls around the world get access to good schools and further education.

Michelle Obama

3 THE CONSTITUTION AND THE PRESIDENCY

Ever since the founding of the United States, the Constitution has laid out the powers, duties, and responsibilities of the president—the holder of the most important office in the country. Over the years, further constitutional changes have been made to define what the president can do, how the president is elected, and who can vote in the presidential elections.

WHERE HISTORY WAS WRITTEN
Independence Hall in Philadelphia
has been the home of many important
historical events. Both the Declaration of
Independence and the US Constitution
were signed in the building.

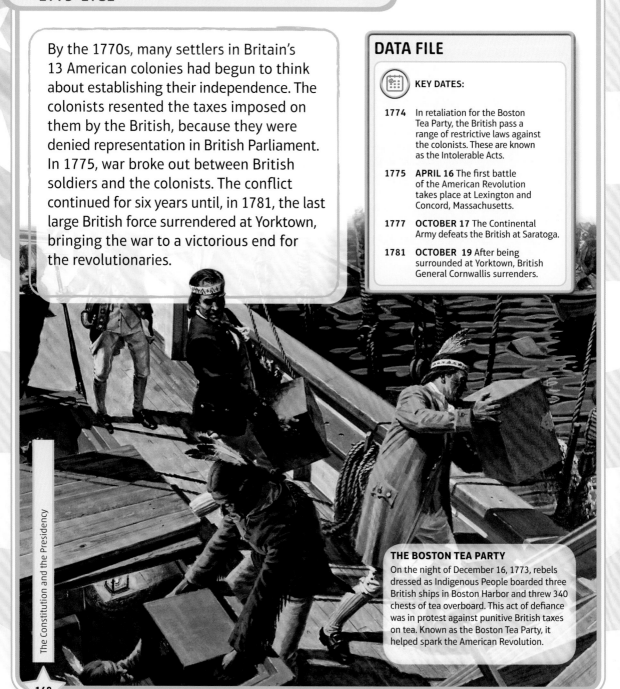

THE AMERICAN
REVOLUTION
1775–1781

By the 1770s, many settlers in Britain's 13 American colonies had begun to think about establishing their independence. The colonists resented the taxes imposed on them by the British, because they were denied representation in British Parliament. In 1775, war broke out between British soldiers and the colonists. The conflict continued for six years until, in 1781, the last large British force surrendered at Yorktown, bringing the war to a victorious end for the revolutionaries.

DATA FILE

KEY DATES:

1774 In retaliation for the Boston Tea Party, the British pass a range of restrictive laws against the colonists. These are known as the Intolerable Acts.

1775 **APRIL 16** The first battle of the American Revolution takes place at Lexington and Concord, Massachusetts.

1777 **OCTOBER 17** The Continental Army defeats the British at Saratoga.

1781 **OCTOBER 19** After being surrounded at Yorktown, British General Cornwallis surrenders.

THE BOSTON TEA PARTY

On the night of December 16, 1773, rebels dressed as Indigenous People boarded three British ships in Boston Harbor and threw 340 chests of tea overboard. This act of defiance was in protest against punitive British taxes on tea. Known as the Boston Tea Party, it helped spark the American Revolution.

The Constitution and the Presidency

THE DECLARATION OF
INDEPENDENCE
1776

During the Revolution, the Second Continental Congress met in Philadelphia in June 1776 and decided to begin drafting a Declaration of Independence. Thomas Jefferson authored the first draft of this document, which listed American grievances against the British and the rights the colonists were claiming for themselves. On July 4, 1776, the Declaration officially came into effect, declaring the United States an independent nation.

DATA FILE

KEY FIGURES: Thomas Jefferson, John Adams, Benjamin Franklin

ADOPTED AT: Second Continental Congress, Philadelphia

NUMBER OF STATES SIGNED BY: 13

CURRENT LOCATION: National Archives, Washington, D.C.

THE COMMITTEE OF FIVE
The Continental Congress appointed a five-member committee to draft the Declaration of Independence, which comprised John Adams, Roger Sherman, Robert R. Livingston, Thomas Jefferson, and Benjamin Franklin (shown here from left to right).

American Revolution/Declaration of Independence

After running the government based on the Articles of Confederation for several years, in May 1797 delegates from 12 states met at the Constitutional Convention in Philadelphia, Pennsylvania, to formalize how it would operate. There was much debate between those who wanted a strong central government—including Alexander Hamilton, who coauthored the Federalist Papers—and those who wanted individual states to retain many or most powers. However, after a period of almost four months, 39 delegates signed a final draft. This document established a system of federal governance for the states, and was declared "the supreme law of the land."

DATA FILE

 KEY FIGURES: James Madison, Alexander Hamilton

 DATE SIGNED: September 17, 1787

 NUMBER OF PARTICIPATING STATES: 55 delegates from 12 states. Rhode Island was the only one of the 13 colonies not to send delegates.

 DATE RATIFIED BY ALL STATES: May 29, 1790

The Constitution and the Presidency

At **4,400 words**, the **US Constitution** is the **shortest** of all the world's **written national constitutions**.

SIGNING THE CONSTITUTION

In this image, the delegates are pictured gathering to sign the Constitution. After it was signed, the document needed nine states to ratify it to go into effect, which happened on June 21, 1788, when New Hampshire ratified it.

PRESIDENTIAL
POWERS

The powers of the presidency were laid down in the Constitution by the Founding Fathers. They intended for the president to act as the country's chief executive, and gave him or her the ability to sign congressional legislation into law, and to veto (reject) any legislation he or she does not approve of. The president also has an important international role as a figurehead for the country, and can make treaties with foreign states. Other presidential powers include the ability to appoint ambassadors and Supreme Court justices, and to grant pardons. Although not explicitly mentioned in the Constitution, the president may also issue executive orders that have the force of law.

FIRST INAUGURATION
George Washington began the tradition of an inaugural address given by the president. He is shown here taking the oath of office at his inauguration at Federal Hall, New York City, on April 30, 1789.

COMMANDER-IN-CHIEF

The Constitution appoints the president as commander-in-chief of the armed forces, but also gives Congress the sole power to declare war. Although Congress has granted some presidents additional powers during wartime, such as President Roosevelt during World War II, the original overlapping powers have often caused confusion. In 1973, Congress passed the War Powers Resolution to address this, which limited the president's ability to send troops overseas without congressional approval.

President **Franklin D. Roosevelt** issued the **most executive orders**—a total of **3,522**.

DATA FILE

REQUIREMENTS: Must be a natural-born citizen, aged 35 or older, and have been a resident in the United States for 14 years.

TIME IN OFFICE: Term of four years, maximum of two terms (since 1951)

ORDER OF SUCCESSION: Should the president die or leave office unexpectedly, he or she is succeeded first by the vice president, and then in the following order by the Speaker of the House of Representatives, president pro tempore of the Senate, and Secretary of State.

SALARY: $400,000 (since 2001)

PRESIDENTIAL
ELECTIONS

Early presidential elections were simple, with small groups of free white men, the only Americans allowed to serve as electors, voting at local gatherings. The electorate increased to include all men in 1870 and white women in 1920. Many potential voters were still disenfranchised until the late 20th century. Today, the American electorate includes around 215 million potential voters. Parties often spend vast sums of money to campaign for their candidates on many different media platforms. The 2012 campaign cost the two main parties around $2.6 billion in total with television ads and social media campaigns driving much of the cost. Upon winning, the successful candidate does not take office immediately; there is a two-month transition period.

DATA FILE

HELD: Every four years
ELECTION DAY: First Tuesday after the first Monday in November
INAUGURATION DAY: March 4 until 1933; January 20 since 1937

PRESIDENTIAL OATH:
"I do solemnly swear (or affirm) that I will faithfully execute the Office of President of the United States, and will to the best of my ability, preserve, protect and defend the Constitution of the United States."

REELECTION CAMPAIGN
Presidential candidates often hold big events to attract supporters. Pictured here, President George H. W. Bush and his wife Barbara campaign for reelection in 1992.

THE ELECTORAL SYSTEM

COUNTING THE VOTES
In this image, both houses of Congress meet to count the Electoral College votes from the 2008 election. A candidate needs 270 electoral votes to be declared the winner.

Since the presidential elections of 1796, candidates have been chosen by their political party. From 1901, this has been done through primaries and caucuses—events where party members vote for whom they would like to represent them. Candidates from each party then compete against each other. However, the popular vote does not directly decide the winner. In most states, the candidate who wins the vote gets to appoint their supporters as that state's electors. The appointed electors from all the states form an Electoral College, and they then vote for the future president.

DATA FILE

MAIN PRESIDENTIAL PARTIES:
Republican and Democrat

DATE OF ELECTORAL COLLEGE VOTE COUNT:
January 6

ORIGINAL SIZE OF ELECTORAL COLLEGE (1789): 69 electors
CURRENT SIZE OF ELECTORAL COLLEGE (2020): 538 electors

☞ Political Parties **pp.200–201**

Presidential Elections/The Electoral System

THE PRESIDENT AND
CONGRESS

Established in 1787, Congress comprises two houses: the Senate and the House of Representatives. Through a system of checks, put in place by the Constitution, the powers of Congress and the president are balanced. The president can veto legislation proposed by Congress, while presidential appointments and treaties must be approved by the Senate. Congress also has to approve the federal budget, which is submitted by the president. When Congress is controlled by a party different from that of the president, initiatives proposed by one are often blocked by the other—leading to a state known as "gridlock."

DATA FILE

CONSTITUTIONAL PROVISION: "Every Bill which shall have passed the House of Representatives and the Senate, shall, before it become a Law, be presented to the President of the United States; If he approve he shall sign it, but if not he shall return it, with his Objections to that House in which it shall have originated."

DATE OF FIRST PRESIDENTIAL VETO: April 5, 1792 (by George Washington)
NUMBER OF PRESIDENTIAL VETOES: 2,582 (to September 2020)

PRESIDENTS EXERCISING LARGEST NUMBER OF VETOES:
Franklin D. Roosevelt: 635
Grover Cleveland: 414
Harry S. Truman: 250

PRESIDENTIAL VETO

Although presidents have the power to veto bills that they disapprove of, a presidential veto can be overridden by a two-thirds vote in both the Senate and the House of Representatives. In 1996, an act passed by Congress also granted presidents the power of line-item veto (to veto specific parts of a bill). However, the Supreme Court later ruled this unconstitutional and Bill Clinton remains the only president to have exercised this power.

The President and Congress

THE BILL OF
RIGHTS

1791

After the Constitution was signed, many in Congress felt it did not sufficiently protect the personal liberties of citizens. This group—called the Anti-Federalists—lobbied for amendments to guarantee individual rights and freedoms. Responding to these calls, James Madison proposed a list of changes, and in 1791, ten amendments were introduced to the Constitution. Collectively known as the Bill of Rights, these cover a range of entitlements, from freedom of speech to the right to trial by jury.

DATA FILE

KEY PROVISIONS:
First Amendment: Right to freedom of speech and religion.
Second Amendment: Right to bear arms.
Fifth Amendment: Right to refuse to give evidence against oneself in court.
Sixth Amendment: Right to trial by jury.
Tenth Amendment: All powers not given by the Constitution to the federal government to remain with the states.

FIRST INTRODUCTION:
July 21, 1789

CONGRESSIONAL APPROVAL:
September 25, 1789

**DATE OF RATIFICATION
(10 ARTICLES):** December 15, 1791

THE NATIONAL ARCHIVES

Altogether, 14 handwritten copies of the Bill of Rights were made—one for the federal government and one for each of the 13 states. Today, the American government's copy is housed in the National Archives in Washington, D.C., where visitors can view the original document on display.

The Bill of Rights

The Bill of Rights

THE CIVIL WAR

1861–1865

In 1861, a bitter conflict threatened to destroy the Union. Strongly in favor of slavery, seven Southern states left the Union and established the Confederate States of America. They feared the election of Abraham Lincoln would mean a constriction of their right to hold slaves They later attacked Fort Sumter in Charleston Harbor, South Carolina, beginning the Civil War and causing four more states to leave the Union and join the Confederacy. Fighting escalated quickly, but despite the efforts of talented generals such as Robert E. Lee, the Confederacy remained a weaker force. After the 1862 Emancipation Proclamation, Black soldiers joined the Union forces, helping cement their victory at Gettysburg in 1863. This left the South on the defensive, and its last large force surrendered in April 1865. By the end of the war, around 620,000 soldiers had lost their lives.

DATA FILE

UNION STATES: 20
CONFEDERATE STATES: 11

KEY DATES:

1861 **APRIL** Confederate troops attack Fort Sumter, South Carolina.

1861 **JULY** The first Battle of Bull Run, Virginia, is fought.

1862 **DECEMBER** Confederate troops win a decisive victory at the Battle of Fredericksburg, Virginia.

1863 **JULY** The Union wins the bloodiest battle of the Civil War at Gettysburg, Pennsylvania.

1865 **APRIL** General Robert E. Lee surrenders to General Ulysses S. Grant at Appomattox Court House, Virginia.

THE CONFEDERATE STATES

Formed in February 1861, the Confederate States of America included the 11 Southern states that had left the Union. Its first (and only) president was Jefferson Davis, who had previously been a senator from Mississippi as well as Secretary of War. This painting depicts his inauguration in Montgomery, Alabama, in February 1861.

THE SIEGE OF VICKSBURG

Union troops attacked the Confederate defensive lines during the Siege of Vicksburg, Mississippi, in 1863. The siege ended with the capture of the last Confederate stronghold on the Mississippi River.

The Civil War

13TH AMENDMENT
ABOLITION OF SLAVERY
1865

The issue of whether or not to allow slavery had plagued the United States since its foundation, and ultimately led to the Civil War. President Lincoln's Emancipation Proclamation of 1863 freed many slaves, but it did not legally abolish slavery. As the Civil War drew to a close, the nation debated the need for a new constitutional amendment to outlaw this practice. Although there was fierce opposition, the 13th Amendment was successfully passed in January 1865.

14TH AMENDMENT

The abolition of slavery did not stop discrimination against formerly enslaved people. Congress passed a Civil Rights Act in 1866, but this did not sufficiently protect the legal rights of Black people. Finally, the 14th Amendment was passed to guarantee all American citizens equal protection under the law. This came into effect in 1868, but the country still struggles with adhering to it today.

The Constitution and the Presidency

MAIN PROVISION: "Neither slavery nor involuntary servitude, except as a punishment for crime whereof the party shall have been duly convicted, shall exist within the United States, or any place subject to their jurisdiction."

FIRST INTRODUCTION: December 14, 1863

CONGRESSIONAL APPROVAL: January 31, 1865

DATE OF RATIFICATION: December 6, 1865

Around **4 million enslaved people** were **freed** by the **passing** of the **13th Amendment**.

CELEBRATING LIBERTY

Formerly enslaved people celebrate the passing of the 13th Amendment, displaying copies of newspapers that proclaimed the news of their freedom. This is often celebrated on Juneteenth.

Abolition of Slavery

15TH AMENDMENT
VOTING RIGHTS
1870

In 1870, the Republicans helped pass the 15th Amendment, granting the right to vote to all men, regardless of their race or color. This law complemented the 13th and 14th amendments, which had abolished slavery and extended citizenship to Black people. However, "Jim Crow" laws were passed in the Southern states that denied Black people equal rights. States imposed conditions on voters, such as taxes or literacy tests, that prevented many Black people from exercising their right to vote, especially in the South.

By February 1870, **29 of the 37 states** had ratified the **15th Amendment**.

DATA FILE

MAIN PROVISION: "The right of citizens of the United States to vote shall not be denied or abridged by the United States or by any State on account of race, color, or previous condition of servitude."

FIRST INTRODUCTION: January 30, 1869

DATE OF RATIFICATION: February 3, 1870

Voting Rights

18TH AMENDMENT
PROHIBITION

1919

In the late 19th century, concern that drinking alcohol caused violence led to calls for it to be banned. Many states passed legislation outlawing alcohol, and the Anti-Saloon League led a campaign for an amendment to ban it nationally. The passing of the 18th Amendment and the Volstead Act, which specified the types of alcohol that were banned, began an era known as "Prohibition." However, a lack of money to pay for inspectors to enforce this ban led to the growth of "speakeasies"—illegal bars where alcohol could still be bought. Crime also rose, as gangsters such as Al Capone in Chicago took over the illegal alcohol trade.

DATA FILE

 MAIN PROVISION: "After one year from the ratification of this article the manufacture, sale, or transportation of intoxicating liquors within, the importation thereof into, or the exportation thereof from the United States and all territory subject to the jurisdiction thereof for beverage purposes is hereby prohibited."

 FIRST INTRODUCTION:
August 1, 1917

 CONGRESSIONAL APPROVAL:
December 18, 1917

 DATE OF RATIFICATION:
January 16, 1919

ILLEGAL TRADE
In New York City, there were tens of thousands of speakeasies during the Prohibition era. In this image, police watch as government agents pour barrels of illegal alcohol down the sewers.

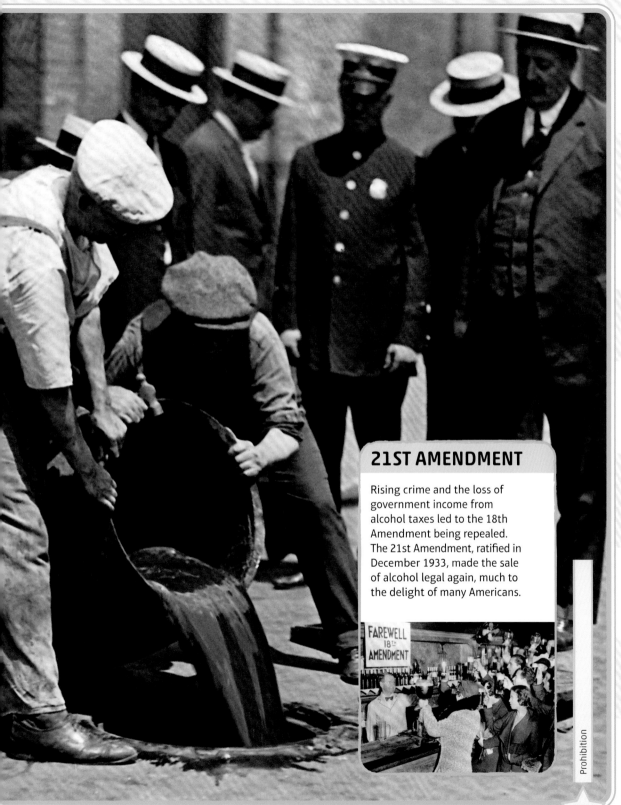

21ST AMENDMENT

Rising crime and the loss of government income from alcohol taxes led to the 18th Amendment being repealed. The 21st Amendment, ratified in December 1933, made the sale of alcohol legal again, much to the delight of many Americans.

FAREWELL 18TH AMENDMENT

Prohibition

19TH AMENDMENT
WOMEN'S SUFFRAGE
1920

Although during the 19th century voting rights had been extended to many men, American women were still not allowed to vote. The struggle to obtain this right—known as suffrage—began in 1848 when a women's rights convention in Seneca Falls, New York, listed it as a fundamental right in their "Declaration of Sentiments." Women's groups began to lobby for a constitutional amendment, but it took many years for it to pass. Many women already had been granted voting rights by their states, but it was only on November 2, 1920, that American women were given the federal right to vote. Still, racially-motivated means of disenfranchisement effectively kept many women of color from the polls until the Voting Rights Act of 1965 was passed, prohibiting racial discrimination in voting.

CELEBRATING VICTORY

A crowd cheers women's suffrage campaigner Alice Paul as she unfurls a banner to celebrate the ratification of the 19th Amendment by Tennessee. This meant that the amendment had been ratified by enough states to come into effect.

The Constitution and the Presidency

DATA FILE

MAIN PROVISION: "The right of citizens of the United States to vote shall not be denied or abridged by the United States or by any State on account of sex."

FIRST INTRODUCTION: January 1878

CONGRESSIONAL APPROVAL: June 4, 1919

DATE OF RATIFICATION: August 18, 1920

VOTES FOR ALL WOMEN

Despite the efforts of suffrage activists such as Nannie Burroughs (pictured), many women, including Indigenous, Black, Asian, and Latinx women, were not able to vote until later in the 20th century, either because they were not regarded as citizens or because they were effectively barred from voting.

Women's Suffrage

22ND AMENDMENT
TWO-TERM LIMIT
1951

The Constitution set no limit on the number of terms a president could serve, but, following the example of George Washington, it had become customary to serve only two terms at most. When Franklin D. Roosevelt won election to a fourth term in 1944, it sparked a heated debate in Congress. The Democrats argued that the people's right to choose a president should not be restricted. The Republican argument, that the presidency should not be dominated by one person, won out and led to the 22nd Amendment, which barred presidents from serving for more than two terms.

DATA FILE

 MAIN PROVISION: "No person shall be elected to the office of the President more than twice, and no person who has held the office of President, or acted as President, for more than two years of a term to which some other person was elected President shall be elected to the office of the President more than once."

 CONGRESSIONAL APPROVAL: March 24, 1947

 DATE OF RATIFICATION: February 27, 1951

The Constitution and the Presidency

ROOSEVELT FOR VICTORY
A crowd in Chicago carry placards calling for the reelection of Franklin D. Roosevelt during the 1944 election campaign, which ended with him winning an unprecedented fourth term in office.

26TH AMENDMENT
RIGHT TO VOTE AT 18
1971

The Constitution had set the voting age at 21. However, resentment built up during the Vietnam War when young Americans could be called up to serve in the war at 18, but were still not allowed to vote. After the Supreme Court ruled in 1970 that 18–20-year-olds should be allowed to vote in state elections, Congress moved to pass a constitutional amendment to allow them to do so in federal elections. The amendment was ratified just 107 days after its congressional approval, faster than any other amendment to the Constitution.

DATA FILE

 MAIN PROVISION: "The right of citizens of the United States, who are eighteen years of age or older, to vote shall not be denied or abridged by the United States or by any State on account of age."

 FIRST INTRODUCTION: March 10, 1971

 CONGRESSIONAL APPROVAL: March 23, 1971

 DATE OF RATIFICATION: July 1, 1971

REGISTERING TO VOTE
Students at Westchester High School, California, line up to register to vote in 1971. The slogan "Old enough to fight, old enough to vote" had been key in winning them this right.

4 PRESIDENTIAL PLACES AND VEHICLES

As the demands of the office have become more complex, presidents have been granted a variety of facilities to assist them in performing their job, including specialized offices, such as the West Wing. Presidents have also used residences and retreats outside Washington, D.C., and a series of official aircraft and land vehicles to transport them securely.

WELCOMING THE PRESIDENT

President Obama's official car and a convoy of security wait to greet him as he arrives in Hanover, Germany, on Air Force One.

THE WHITE HOUSE

The White House is the official residence of the president and houses his or her personal and executive offices. Work on the building began in 1792, during Washington's presidency, but was completed only in 1800, when John and Abigail Adams became the first presidential couple to live in the White House. Its first major renovation happened after the War of 1812, and in 1902, Theodore Roosevelt spent more than $500,000 on refurbishments. Over the years, many presidents and first ladies have redecorated the interior of the White House according to their tastes.

The southern facade

The **White House** has **132 rooms**, **35 bathrooms**, eight staircases, and three elevators.

THE BURNING OF WASHINGTON, D.C.

In August 1814, during the War of 1812, British troops occupied Washington, D.C., and set fire to the White House, completely destroying its interior. It took three years to complete the repairs before James and Dolley Madison could move back in.

DATA FILE

YEAR COMPLETED: 1800

ARCHITECT: James Hoban

LOCATION: 1600 Pennsylvania Avenue NW, Washington, D.C.

COST TO BUILD: $232,000

The White House

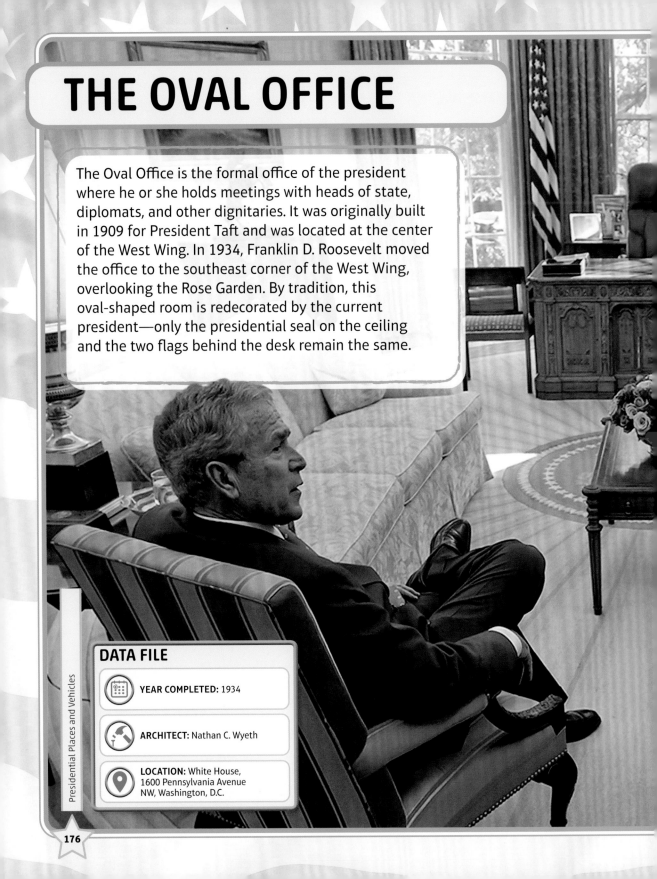

THE OVAL OFFICE

The Oval Office is the formal office of the president where he or she holds meetings with heads of state, diplomats, and other dignitaries. It was originally built in 1909 for President Taft and was located at the center of the West Wing. In 1934, Franklin D. Roosevelt moved the office to the southeast corner of the West Wing, overlooking the Rose Garden. By tradition, this oval-shaped room is redecorated by the current president—only the presidential seal on the ceiling and the two flags behind the desk remain the same.

DATA FILE

YEAR COMPLETED: 1934

ARCHITECT: Nathan C. Wyeth

LOCATION: White House, 1600 Pennsylvania Avenue NW, Washington, D.C.

Each **departing president** leaves a **note** in the Oval Office for his or her **successor**, offering some **advice**.

PRESIDENTIAL MEETING

Shortly after winning the 2008 election, Barack Obama meets with sitting president George W. Bush in the Oval Office. Presidents often confer with their predecessors on the important issues of the day.

The Oval Office

THE WEST WING

The West Wing is the official presidential workplace. It contains a variety of offices, such as the Oval Office, the Cabinet Office—where the president meets with members of the Cabinet—and the Situation Room, which is used as a center for emergency operations. The construction of the West Wing began after Theodore Roosevelt realized the executive mansion did not offer enough room to carry out all presidential duties. The building has been enlarged several times and has become the hub of activity at the White House.

DATA FILE

 YEAR COMPLETED: 1902

 ARCHITECTS: McKim, Mead & White

 LOCATION: 1600 Pennsylvania Avenue NW, Washington, D.C.

Outside view

PRESIDENTIAL ADVISORS
President Lyndon B. Johnson meets with the National Security Council and other officials on October 31, 1968.

Presidential Places and Vehicles

EISENHOWER EXECUTIVE
OFFICE BUILDING

Located opposite the West Wing, the Eisenhower Executive Office Building houses the offices of the vice president and the National Security Council. Originally built for the State, War, and Navy Departments, it took 17 years to be completed. It was gradually acquired by the White House between 1939 and 1949. Decorated with elaborate columns, the building has a distinctive architectural style, and was described by author Mark Twain as "the ugliest building in America."

DATA FILE

 YEAR COMPLETED: 1888

 ARCHITECT: Alfred B. Mullett

 LOCATION: 1650 Pennsylvania Avenue NW, Washington, D.C.

The West Wing/Eisenhower Executive Office Building

BLAIR HOUSE

The presidential guest house for visiting heads of state, Blair House is located across the street from the White House. Originally built in 1824, it was acquired in 1942 by President Franklin D. Roosevelt. The building is made up of four connected townhouses, with more than 120 rooms and a staff of 18 full-time employees. Notable guests who have stayed at Blair House include British Prime Minister Margaret Thatcher, French President Charles de Gaulle, and Russian President Vladimir Putin. In addition to hosting foreign dignitaries, the building is also used as a venue for events and becomes a residence for presidents-elect in the days prior to their inauguration.

Whenever **foreign leaders** stay in Blair House, the **flag of their country** flies outside the building.

FIRST BUILT: 1824
LAST REFURBISHED IN: 1989

ARCHITECTS: Mendel, Mesick, Cohen, Waite, Hall Architects

LOCATION: Pennsylvania Avenue NW, Washington, D.C.

THE TRUMAN WHITE HOUSE

In 1948, during the presidency of Harry S. Truman, it was found that the White House needed extensive renovations. The president and his family moved into Blair House and lived there for the next four years. During this time, it was popularly known as the "Truman White House."

Blair House

CAMP DAVID

Set in the mountains of Maryland, Camp David provides a weekend home for presidents. It was originally built as a camp for federal employees, but in 1942, Franklin D. Roosevelt had it remodeled as a presidential retreat. Camp David is also used by presidents to host foreign heads of state. In 1978, President Carter used it as the venue for the historic peace talks between the Egyptian President Anwar Sadat and the Israeli Prime Minister Menachem Begin.

DATA FILE

YEAR COMPLETED: 1938

CONSTRUCTED BY: Works Progress Administration

LOCATION: Catoctin Mountain Park, Frederick County, Maryland

President **Eisenhower** named Camp David **after** both **his father** and **his grandson**.

NUMBER ONE
OBSERVATORY CIRCLE

Acquired by the federal government in 1974, Number One Observatory Circle is the official residence of the vice president and his or her family. The mansion was built in 1893, and previously housed senior naval officers. Walter Mondale became the first vice president to move into the house in 1977, and since then the building has undergone extensive remodeling. Many vice presidents have even added additional features to the residence, including a swimming pool.

DATA FILE

YEAR COMPLETED: 1893

ARCHITECT: Leon E. Dessez

LOCATION: 3450 Massachusetts Avenue NW, Washington, D.C.

Camp David/Number One Observatory Circle

MOUNT VERNON

Mount Vernon was the private residence of George and Martha Washington. The Virginia estate belonged to George's father, Augustine, who started the construction of a small house there. When George acquired the estate in 1754, he ordered the building of a grander house in the classical Palladian style, modeled on villas in Italy. In the years following his retirement, Washington hosted hundreds of guests at Mount Vernon. The house later fell into disrepair until it was restored by the Mount Vernon Ladies Association in 1858. It is now a National Historic Landmark.

Inside view, 1925

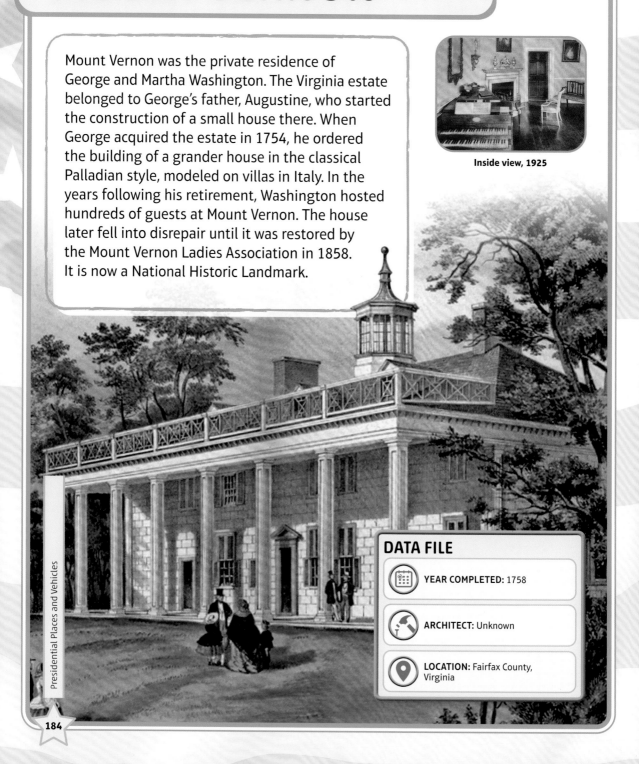

DATA FILE

YEAR COMPLETED: 1758

ARCHITECT: Unknown

LOCATION: Fairfax County, Virginia

MONTICELLO

Inside view—hallway

Monticello was the private home of Thomas Jefferson. A man of many talents, Jefferson designed the house himself and modeled it on the neoclassical style of the villas he saw while serving as ambassador to France. The 33-room house was surrounded by a vast botanic garden, which was used by Jefferson to breed plants and grow many varieties of vegetables. After his death in 1826, Jefferson was buried at Monticello. The property was bought by the Thomas Jefferson Foundation in 1923 and opened to the public.

Monticello was **seized by the Confederacy** during the Civil War.

DATA FILE

 CONSTRUCTION BEGAN: 1769
YEAR COMPLETED: 1809

 DESIGNED BY: Thomas Jefferson

 LOCATION: Albemarle County, Virginia

Mount Vernon/Monticello

MOUNT RUSHMORE

Created as a tribute to the American presidency, Mount Rushmore features the faces of George Washington, Thomas Jefferson, Theodore Roosevelt, and Abraham Lincoln—all carved into a giant granite cliff. South Dakota's state historian, Doane Robinson, commissioned the work in 1923 by Gutzon Borglum, a sculptor famous for large-scale stonework. Using jackhammers, chisels, and dynamite, Borglum carved the four faces for 18 years, leaving their completion to his son Lincoln when he passed away. Not all Americans see the statues as a symbol of democracy. For the Lakota Sioux, the land the monument is built on is sacred, and was taken from them by European settlers.

DATA FILE

PROJECT STARTED: October 1927
WORK COMPLETED: October 1941

DESIGNED BY: Gutzon Borglum

LOCATION: Black Hills, South Dakota

SIZE: Height of each head 60 ft (18 m)

Around **450,000 tons** of **granite** were **blasted** from the rock face to **make** the **statues**.

Mount Rushmore

AIR FORCE ONE

Air Force One is the president's official plane, which is often used for visits overseas. The first Air Force One was a Boeing 707, which was delivered to President Kennedy in 1962. This was later upgraded to a Boeing 747 in 1990. Currently, there are two identical aircraft that serve as presidential planes, each including a conference room, a media room, an operating room, 85 telephones, and a presidential bedroom suite. The call sign "Air Force One" is also used to refer to any plane the president is traveling in.

DATA FILE

 YEAR FIRST USED: 1962

 MADE BY: Boeing

 HOME BASE: Joint Base Andrews, Prince George's County, Maryland

 LENGTH: 250 ft (76 m)

Each official plane stands as tall as a **six-story building**.

Inside view

CADILLAC ONE

In 1939, Franklin D. Roosevelt became the first president to own a specially built state car, called "Sunshine One." The current car, officially designated "Cadillac One," was given to President Obama in 2009. In the wake of President Kennedy's assassination, presidential cars became increasingly well protected, and Cadillac One is designed with five layers of armor. Nicknamed "The Beast" for its sheer size, the car can withstand attacks by chemical weapons, and has secure communication facilities. Cadillac One even has its own plane—a C-17 Globemaster—to airlift it to the place the president is visiting.

DATA FILE

 YEAR FIRST USED: 2009 (current model)

 MADE BY: General Motors

 LENGTH: 18 ft (5.5 m)

The Beast **weighs** more than **15,000 pounds** (6,800 kilograms).

GROUND FORCE ONE

Until 2011, whenever presidents needed to be transported by bus, one was acquired and specially customized. Since this was expensive and did not meet increasing security requirements, the Secret Service commissioned two special armored buses as permanent presidential vehicles. Nicknamed "Ground Force One," these buses have armored exteriors and specially reinforced glass, as well as housing secure communication equipment and an extra supply of the president's blood in case he or she is injured. The buses are even big enough to conduct meetings inside.

DATA FILE

 YEAR FIRST USED: 2012

 MADE BY: Prevost Cars and Hemphill Brothers Coach Company

 LOCATION: Washington, D.C.

 LENGTH: 45 ft (14 m)

The two **Ground Force One** buses cost **$1.1 million** each.

MARINE ONE

Dwight D. Eisenhower was the first president to travel by helicopter, in 1957, and since then presidents have often used them to get around safely. Marine One normally refers to the helicopter carrying the US president, a fleet of which is operated by a squadron of the Marines known as the "Nighthawks." The current models, the VH-60N White Hawk and VH-3D Sea King, carry antimissile systems and allow secure communications. When carrying the president, Marine One flies with several other decoy helicopters at its side.

DATA FILE

 YEAR FIRST USED: 1957

 MADE BY: Sikorsky Aircraft Corporation

 LOCATION: Marine Corps Air Facility, Quantico, Virginia

 LENGTH: 65 ft (20 m)

Ground Force One/Marine One

5
REFERENCE

Find out some amazing behind-the-scenes facts about the nation's presidents—where they came from, their vice presidents, and some of their shocking election victories. Discover also a collection of fun trivia about presidents' hobbies and some of their most famous pets.

US PRESIDENTS
STATE BY STATE

Herbert
Hoover

Gerald R.
Ford

Alaska
1959

Washington
1889

Montana
1889

North Dakota
1889

Oregon
1859

Idaho
1890

Wyoming
1890

South Dakota
1889

Nevada
1864

Utah
1896

Colorado
1876

Nebraska
1867

Kansas
1861

California
1850

Richard
M. Nixon

Arizona
1912

New Mexico
1912

Oklahoma
1907

Texas
1845

Barack
Obama

Most US presidents have come from the eastern states of the country. It was not until 1969 that a president from the west was elected. To date, 21 states have been the birthplace of presidents, with Virginia producing the largest number of presidents—eight.

Hawaii
1959

Dwight D.
Eisenhower

Lyndon B.
Johnson

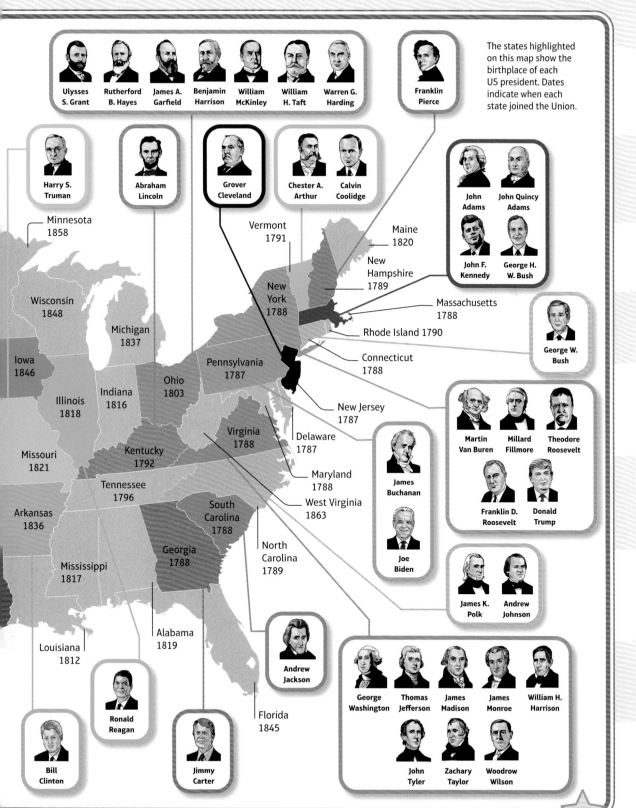

Ulysses S. Grant

Rutherford B. Hayes

James A. Garfield

Benjamin Harrison

William McKinley

William H. Taft

Warren G. Harding

Franklin Pierce

The states highlighted on this map show the birthplace of each US president. Dates indicate when each state joined the Union.

Harry S. Truman

Abraham Lincoln

Grover Cleveland

Chester A. Arthur

Calvin Coolidge

John Adams

John Quincy Adams

John F. Kennedy

George H. W. Bush

Minnesota 1858

Vermont 1791

Maine 1820

New Hampshire 1789

Massachusetts 1788

George W. Bush

Wisconsin 1848

New York 1788

Rhode Island 1790

Michigan 1837

Connecticut 1788

Iowa 1846

Pennsylvania 1787

Illinois 1818

Ohio 1803

Indiana 1816

New Jersey 1787

Martin Van Buren

Millard Fillmore

Theodore Roosevelt

Virginia 1788

Delaware 1787

Missouri 1821

Kentucky 1792

Maryland 1788

Franklin D. Roosevelt

Donald Trump

Tennessee 1796

West Virginia 1863

James Buchanan

Arkansas 1836

South Carolina 1788

North Carolina 1789

Georgia 1788

Joe Biden

Mississippi 1817

James K. Polk

Andrew Johnson

Alabama 1819

Louisiana 1812

Andrew Jackson

George Washington

Thomas Jefferson

James Madison

James Monroe

William H. Harrison

Ronald Reagan

Florida 1845

Bill Clinton

Jimmy Carter

John Tyler

Zachary Taylor

Woodrow Wilson

EXTRAORDINARY ELECTIONS

Presidential elections are always a time of great political excitement. Some elections, however, have provoked more interest than others, either because they have marked a change in the nation's political direction, or because they have been extremely close or controversial.

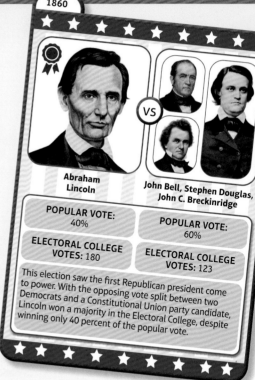

1860

Abraham Lincoln

John Bell, Stephen Douglas, John C. Breckinridge

POPULAR VOTE: 40%

POPULAR VOTE: 60%

ELECTORAL COLLEGE VOTES: 180

ELECTORAL COLLEGE VOTES: 123

This election saw the first Republican president come to power. With the opposing vote split between two Democrats and a Constitutional Union party candidate, Lincoln won a majority in the Electoral College, despite winning only 40 percent of the popular vote.

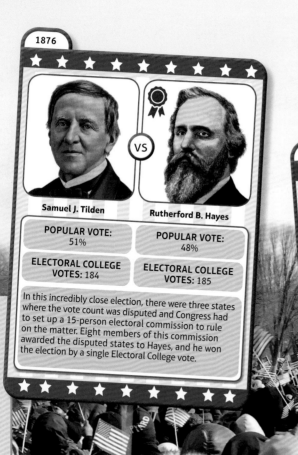

1876

Samuel J. Tilden

Rutherford B. Hayes

POPULAR VOTE: 51%

POPULAR VOTE: 48%

ELECTORAL COLLEGE VOTES: 184

ELECTORAL COLLEGE VOTES: 185

In this incredibly close election, there were three states where the vote count was disputed and Congress had to set up a 15-person electoral commission to rule on the matter. Eight members of this commission awarded the disputed states to Hayes, and he won the election by a single Electoral College vote.

1912

Woodrow Wilson

Theodore Roosevelt, Eugene Debs, William Taft

POPULAR VOTE: 42%

POPULAR VOTE: 56%

ELECTORAL COLLEGE VOTES: 435

ELECTORAL COLLEGE VOTES: 96

In this rare four-way contest, former president Theodore Roosevelt chose to stand for the Progressive Party. This split the Republican vote and allowed Wilson, with his promise of greater rights for workers, to win an overwhelming majority in the Electoral College.

1932

Franklin D. Roosevelt VS **Herbert Hoover**

POPULAR VOTE: 57%	POPULAR VOTE: 40%
ELECTORAL COLLEGE VOTES: 472	ELECTORAL COLLEGE VOTES: 59

During the Great Depression, Franklin D. Roosevelt's promise of a "New Deal" struck a chord with the voters. He amassed an overwhelming Electoral College majority, winning in 42 states. His subsequent four terms in office began a new wave of Democrat dominance.

1948

Thomas E. Dewey Strom Thurmond VS **Harry S. Truman**

POPULAR VOTE: 45%	POPULAR VOTE: 50%
ELECTORAL COLLEGE VOTES: 189	ELECTORAL COLLEGE VOTES: 303

Harry Truman's chances of winning the presidential election of 1948 looked bleak against his Republican rival Thomas Dewey and Strom Thurmond's Dixiecrats, who undermined his chances in the South. Newspaper headlines on election night declared Dewey the victor, but when results came through, it became clear that Truman had won an astonishing victory.

2000

Al Gore VS **George W. Bush**

POPULAR VOTE: 48.5%	POPULAR VOTE: 48%
ELECTORAL COLLEGE VOTES: 266	ELECTORAL COLLEGE VOTES: 271

A hard-fought campaign between Al Gore and George W. Bush ended in one of the most controversial electoral counts in American history. The result hung on disputed ballots from the state of Florida. Gore's supporters wanted these recounted by hand, but the Supreme Court ruled against this. Bush was awarded Florida's electoral votes and won a majority of just five Electoral College votes.

2016

Donald Trump VS **Hillary Clinton**

POPULAR VOTE: 46.1%	POPULAR VOTE: 48.2%
ELECTORAL COLLEGE VOTES: 304	ELECTORAL COLLEGE VOTES: 227

With Hillary Clinton widely predicted to win the election and nearly every poll showing her ahead, election night in 2016 was shocking for supporters of both candidates. While Clinton did win the popular vote by nearly 3 million ballots, Donald Trump swept the Electoral College to win by 304 to Clinton's 227. He won several states by less than 1 percent of the vote. The result stunned many Americans who assumed the first female president would soon take office.

VICE PRESIDENTS

Although recent holders of the office have taken on a more active role, the vice president has few formal powers. However, as president of the Senate, he or she casts a deciding vote in the event of a tie and also succeeds the president if he or she resigns or dies.

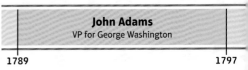

John Adams
VP for George Washington

1789 — 1797

Richard M. Johnson
VP for Martin Van Buren

Daniel D. Tompkins
VP for James Monroe

John C. Calhoun
VP for John Quincy Adams

John C. Calhoun
VP for Andrew Jackson

Martin Van Buren
VP for Andrew Jackson

1825   1829   1832   1833   1837

Hannibal Hamlin
VP for Abraham Lincoln

Andrew Johnson
VP for Abraham Lincoln

Henry Wilson
VP for Ulysses S. Grant

Chester A. Arthur
VP for James A. Garfield

Schuyler Colfax
VP for Ulysses S. Grant

William A. Wheeler
VP for Rutherford B. Hayes

1865   1865 (APRIL)   1869   1873   1875   1877   1881   1881 (SEPTEMBER)

CHARLES W. FAIRBANKS
Fairbanks was a typical vice president of the era who did not attend cabinet meetings and spent much of his time presiding over the Senate.

Calvin Coolidge
VP for Warren G. Harding

Charles W. Fairbanks
VP for Theodore Roosevelt

Thomas R. Marshall
VP for Woodrow Wilson

1905   1909   1912   1913   1921   1923

James S. Sherman
VP for William H. Taft

Lyndon B. Johnson
VP for John F. Kennedy

Alben W. Barkley
VP for Harry S. Truman

Richard M. Nixon
VP for Dwight D. Eisenhower

1949   1953   1961   1963   1965

AL GORE
Gore worked on several issues, including digital technology, the environment, and cutting wasteful bureaucracy.

DICK CHENEY
Cheney was heavily involved in government, particularly in overseeing military and national security plans.

Dan Quayle
VP for George H. W. Bush

Al Gore
VP for Bill Clinton

Dick Cheney
VP for George W. Bush

1989   1993   2001

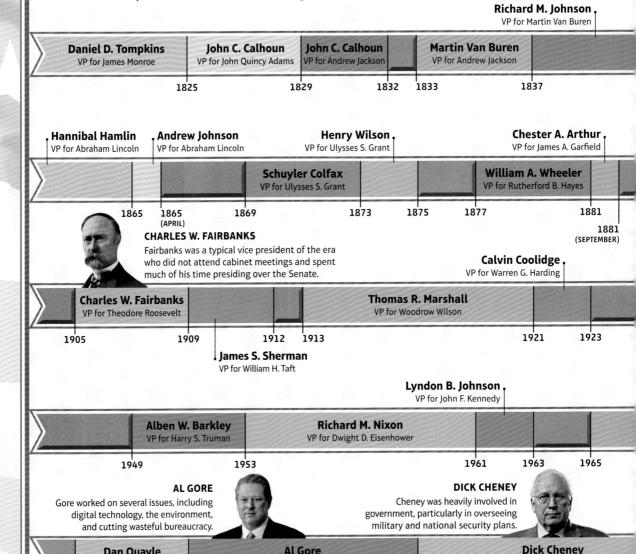

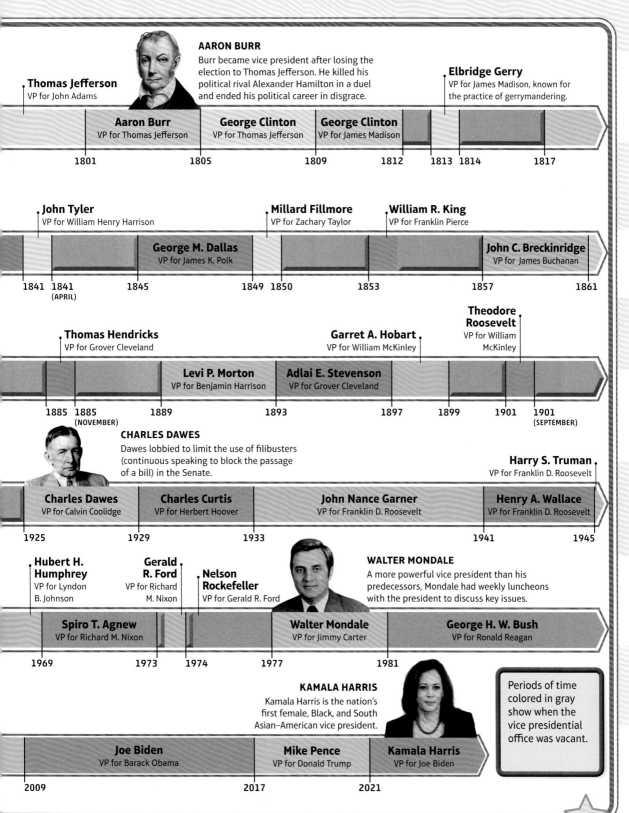

AARON BURR
Burr became vice president after losing the election to Thomas Jefferson. He killed his political rival Alexander Hamilton in a duel and ended his political career in disgrace.

Thomas Jefferson
VP for John Adams

Elbridge Gerry
VP for James Madison, known for the practice of gerrymandering.

Aaron Burr
VP for Thomas Jefferson

George Clinton
VP for Thomas Jefferson

George Clinton
VP for James Madison

1801 | 1805 | 1809 | 1812 | 1813 | 1814 | 1817

John Tyler
VP for William Henry Harrison

Millard Fillmore
VP for Zachary Taylor

William R. King
VP for Franklin Pierce

George M. Dallas
VP for James K. Polk

John C. Breckinridge
VP for James Buchanan

1841 | 1841 (APRIL) | 1845 | 1849 | 1850 | 1853 | 1857 | 1861

Thomas Hendricks
VP for Grover Cleveland

Garret A. Hobart
VP for William McKinley

Theodore Roosevelt
VP for William McKinley

Levi P. Morton
VP for Benjamin Harrison

Adlai E. Stevenson
VP for Grover Cleveland

1885 | 1885 (NOVEMBER) | 1889 | 1893 | 1897 | 1899 | 1901 | 1901 (SEPTEMBER)

CHARLES DAWES
Dawes lobbied to limit the use of filibusters (continuous speaking to block the passage of a bill) in the Senate.

Harry S. Truman
VP for Franklin D. Roosevelt

Charles Dawes
VP for Calvin Coolidge

Charles Curtis
VP for Herbert Hoover

John Nance Garner
VP for Franklin D. Roosevelt

Henry A. Wallace
VP for Franklin D. Roosevelt

1925 | 1929 | 1933 | 1941 | 1945

Hubert H. Humphrey
VP for Lyndon B. Johnson

Gerald R. Ford
VP for Richard M. Nixon

Nelson Rockefeller
VP for Gerald R. Ford

WALTER MONDALE
A more powerful vice president than his predecessors, Mondale had weekly luncheons with the president to discuss key issues.

Spiro T. Agnew
VP for Richard M. Nixon

Walter Mondale
VP for Jimmy Carter

George H. W. Bush
VP for Ronald Reagan

1969 | 1973 | 1974 | 1977 | 1981

KAMALA HARRIS
Kamala Harris is the nation's first female, Black, and South Asian–American vice president.

Periods of time colored in gray show when the vice presidential office was vacant.

Joe Biden
VP for Barack Obama

Mike Pence
VP for Donald Trump

Kamala Harris
VP for Joe Biden

2009 | 2017 | 2021

POLITICAL PARTIES

The only independent president, George Washington, disliked political parties, but they have since become an integral part of US politics. Since the 1796 elections, there have normally been two main parties, and candidates for the presidency have stood on the platform of one of these.

FEDERALISTS

DATE FOUNDED: 1790

PHILOSOPHY: Strong central government.

DATE DISSOLVED: 1824

The Federalists promoted strong economic growth, supported by a powerful central government. In power until 1801, the party faded after its leader Alexander Hamilton was killed, and put forward its last vice presidential candidate in 1820.

WHIGS

DATE FOUNDED: 1834

PHILOSOPHY: The supremacy of Congress over the presidency and high import tariffs.

DATE DISSOLVED: 1856

The Whigs emerged after a split in the Democratic-Republican party. Often a divided party, they supported a wide range of policies, but ultimately fell apart over disagreements on the expansion of slavery into free territories.

DEMOCRATIC-REPUBLICANS

DATE FOUNDED: 1792

PHILOSOPHY: The rights of individual states over the federal government.

DATE DISSOLVED: 1825

The Democratic-Republican party was formed by supporters of Thomas Jefferson, who opposed strong powers for the central government. They aimed to be anti-elitist and championed the interests of farmers and the working class. The party split in the 1820s, and a faction led by Andrew Jackson became the Democrats.

DEMOCRATS

DATE FOUNDED: 1828 to date

PHILOSOPHY: Strong government, social and economic equality, and government involvement in welfare.

Emerging from the split in the Democratic-Republicans, the Democrats championed the poorer classes. They were dominant until 1860, when they split before the Civil War. This led to a period of Republican dominance until Franklin D. Roosevelt's popular New Deal brought them back to power. The modern Democratic party continues to champion a greater role for government and programs to assist less privileged sections of American society.

REPUBLICANS

DATE FOUNDED: 1854 to date

PHILOSOPHY: Limited government, individual freedom, low taxation.

Founded by antislavery activists, the Republicans had their first president in Abraham Lincoln and the Union's victory in the Civil War gave them 70 years of almost unbroken power. However, the Great Depression brought the Republican dominance to an end. Today's Republican party is more socially conservative with a power base in the South and Midwest. It continues to support American business interests and to advocate for stronger national defense.

INDEPENDENT CANDIDATES

Although the United States has a two-party system, minor parties and independents have occasionally made their mark. The highest minor party vote was gained by Theodore Roosevelt's Progressive party in 1912, but others, such as the anti-immigrant "Know Nothing" party in 1856, have also gained a significant percentage of the vote. More recently, independent candidates, such as Ross Perot (right) in 1992, have achieved considerable support due to voter disappointment with the main parties.

PRESIDENTIAL
FUN FACTS

Dwight D. Eisenhower kept three lucky coins in his pocket—a silver dollar, a five-guinea gold coin, and a French franc.

George W. Bush became the **first president** to **complete a marathon**.

William McKinley had a pet **parrot** that he **taught to whistle "Yankee Doodle."**

James Buchanan was **nearsighted in one eye** and **farsighted in the other**, which made him **permanently tilt** his **head to the left**.

Millard Fillmore stood for public office from **three different parties**.

In 1927, **Herbert Hoover appeared** on the **first long-distance television broadcast** in the **US**.

Bill Clinton's hobby was **crossword puzzles**. He even **composed one** for the *New York Times*.

Richard M. Nixon financed his first **congressional campaign** from his **winnings at poker**.

George H. W. Bush celebrated his **90th birthday** by making a **parachute jump**.

At **5 ft 4 in**, James Madison was the **shortest president**.

Woodrow Wilson is the **only president** to have a **PhD**

Before becoming president, **Ronald Reagan costarred** in a movie with a **chimpanzee** named **Peggy**.

As well as having his own pets, **Calvin Coolidge** was **given** a **wallaby**, a **pygmy hippo**, a **black bear**, and a **pair of lion cubs** by foreign dignitaries.

Thomas Jefferson invented the first **swivel chair**.

John Quincy Adams kept an **alligator** as a **pet**.

Franklin D. Roosevelt was a **stamp collector** and **approved** the **design** of over **200 stamps**.

The **teddy bear** was **named after Theodore Roosevelt**.

Abraham Lincoln was the **first president** to have a **beard**, and was the **tallest at 6 ft 4 in**.

Barack Obama collected Spider-Man and Conan the Barbarian **comics**.

GLOSSARY

Abolitionist
A person who called for an end to slavery in the United States.

Act
A law that has been passed by Congress and has come into effect.

Amendment
A change to the Constitution of the United States. To come into effect, this must be passed by Congress, and then be ratified by three-fourths of all the states.

Anarchist
A person who believes that all forms of central government are unjust and who is often prepared to use any means to overthrow the government.

Budget
The spending plans of a government for a set period of time, showing how much it intends to spend and how much it expects to raise in taxes.

Cabinet
The most senior government officials appointed by the president. They are generally in charge of government departments such as the Treasury.

Capitalism
An economic system where the means of production (such as businesses, factories, and farms) are privately owned with a view to making a profit.

Civil Rights
The right of citizens of a country to equal treatment under the law, regardless of gender, race, political beliefs, sexuality, or religion.

Civil Service
The people who are employed by the government to run its various departments.

Cold War
The political confrontation between the United States and the Soviet Union (now Russia), 1947–1991.

Communism
An economic system in which the means of production are owned by the government and wealth is distributed by it.

The Confederacy
The 11 states that broke away from the Union and formed an independent country in 1861. It was dissolved in 1865 at the end of the Civil War.

Congress
The two houses that make up the legislative (law-making)

branch of US government. It oversees the national budget and can also impeach the president for misconduct.

Constitutional
When something is allowed by the Constitution. Any acts or measures that are not permitted under the Constitution are referred to as unconstitutional.

Executive
The branch of the US government responsible for implementing and enforcing laws, headed by the president.

Federal
Matters that are under the control of central government, as opposed to individual states.

Founding Fathers
The group of people who played an important role in the foundation of the United States—in particular, those who attended the Constitutional Convention of 1787.

Governor
The head of a state government within the United States.

House of Representatives
One of the two houses of the United States Congress. Members are elected for a two-year term and the number representing each state varies according to the state's population.

Impeachment
The process by which a president or vice president can be removed from office when accused of misconduct. It involves a trial by members of the Senate.

Inauguration
The ceremony at which a newly elected president takes the oath of office and begins his or her presidency.

Inflation
The increase in the level of prices in a country compared to the previous year. When inflation is high, people have to pay far more for the same goods.

Legislation
Measures proposed by the government that are then passed by Congress and become law.

National Debt
The total amount of money owed by a government as a result of spending more than it raises in taxation.

Nationalist
A person who believes that the political and economic interests of their own country are more important than others and who often opposes international cooperation between nations.

Primary (or Caucus)
An election in a state by which delegates are chosen who will then (together with those from other states) select a party's candidate for the presidential election.

Ratification
The process by which an amendment to the Constitution must be accepted by three-fourths of all US states before it can come into effect.

Recession
A period when the economy of a country goes into decline.

Reconstruction
The period from 1865–1877 during which the states that had formed the Confederacy were placed under military supervision by the federal government, before being readmitted to the Union.

Secession
The act of withdrawing part of a country from the control of the central government, as done by the 11 Southern states who left the Union in 1861 and 1862.

Segregation
The practice of enforced separation of people of different races in schools, workplaces, restaurants, and so on.

Senate
One of the two houses of the United States Congress. Each state is represented by two senators who are elected for a six-year term.

States' rights
Those rights and powers that are held by individual states as opposed to the federal government.

Suffrage
The right to vote in elections, which has been gradually extended to almost all American citizens over 18.

Supreme Court
The highest court in the United States, known as SCOTUS. Its nine justices hear appeals from lower courts and decide whether decisions made by them are constitutional or unconstitutional.

Tariff
A tax or duty placed by a government on imports or exports, as a means to control trade or raise money.

Territory
Historically, a region under the control of the federal government, but which is not yet a state.

The Union
The group of states that came together to form the United States, often used to refer to those that did not secede during the Civil War.

Veto
The power of a president to reject any bill that has been passed by Congress.

INDEX

ACKNOWLEDGMENTS

Reviewer for the Smithsonian:
Bethanee Bemis, Museum Specialist, Division of Political History, National Museum of American History

Smithsonian Enterprises:
Kealy Gordon, Product Development Manager; Jill Corcoran, Director, Licensed Publishing; Janet Archer, DMM, Ecom and D-to-C; Carol LeBlanc, President

The publisher would like to thank the following people for their help with making the book:
Rupa Rao for editorial assistance; Sneha Murchavade for picture research; Neeraj Bhatia for hi-res assistance; and Carron Brown for proofreading and indexing.

Picture Credits
The publisher would like to thank the following for their kind permission to reproduce their photographs:

(Key: a-above; b-below/bottom; c-center; f-far; l-left; r-right; t-top)

2 Dreamstime.com: Timehacker (l). **3 Dreamstime.com:** Brandon Seidel. **4 Alamy Stock Photo:** IanDagnall Computing (bc); Painting / White House Historical Association (bl). **Getty Images:** Bettmann (br); Saul Loeb / AFP (cla). **5 Alamy Stock Photo:** GL Archive (bl). **Getty Images:** Brooks Kraft LLC / Corbis (cra). **6 Alamy Stock Photo:** Holger Hollemann / dpa (cra). **Getty Images:** MPI (cla). **6–7 Alamy Stock Photo:** Mervyn Rees (b). **7 Alamy Stock Photo:** Allstar Picture Library (cla). **Getty Images:** Raymond Boyd (cra). **8–9 Getty Images:** Saul Loeb / AFP. **10–11 Alamy Stock Photo:** Tomas Abad. **Dreamstime.com:** Brett Critchley (All spreads). **12–13 Alamy Stock Photo:** Photo Researchers, Inc. **14–15 Courtesy National Gallery of Art, Washington.** **15 Library of Congress, Washington, DC:** S.W. Fores, 1798 June 1 / LC-DIG-ppmsca-31156 (cr). **16 Alamy Stock Photo:** Painting / White House Historical Association. **17 Alamy Stock Photo:** Granger Historical Picture Archive. **18–19 The Art Archive:** Granger Collection. **20 Getty Images:** DeAgostini. **21 Alamy Stock Photo:** Archive Images. **22–23 Alamy Stock Photo:** Granger Historical Picture Archive. **24–25 Getty Images:** GraphicaArtis. **24 Getty Images:** Bettmann (bc). **26–27 Mary Evans Picture Library:** Everett Collection. **28 Alamy Stock Photo:** IanDagnall Computing. **29 Alamy Stock Photo:** Granger Historical Picture Archive. **30–31 Getty Images:** Universal History Archive. **31 Alamy Stock Photo:** Granger Historical Picture Archive (br). **32–33 Alamy Stock Photo:** IanDagnall Computing. **33 Alamy Stock Photo:** Prisma Archivo (tr). **34 Alamy Stock Photo:** IanDagnall Computing. **35 Alamy Stock Photo:** Granger Historical Picture Archive. **36–37 Bridgeman Images:** Brown, William G. Jr. (19th Century) / © Chicago History Museum, USA. **38–39 Getty Images:** Universal History Archive. **39 Getty Images:** Bettmann (br). **40 Alamy Stock Photo:** IanDagnall Computing. **41 Alamy Stock Photo:** Granger Historical Picture Archive. **42–43 Alamy Stock Photo:** North Wind Picture Archives. **43 Getty Images:** Kean Collection (tr). **44–45 Getty Images:** Library Of Congress. **46 Getty Images:** MPI. **47 Getty Images:** Fine Art Images / Heritage Images. **48 Alamy Stock Photo:** The Art Archive. **49 Alamy Stock Photo:** North Wind Picture Archives. **50–51 Getty Images:** VCG Wilson / Corbis. **51 Alamy Stock Photo:** Everett Collection Inc (br). **52 Library of Congress, Washington, DC:** LC-USZ62-13019. **53 Alamy Stock Photo:** North Wind Picture Archives. **54 Library of Congress, Washington, DC:** LC-DIG-cwpbh-03741 / Brady-Handy Collection. **55 Getty Images:** Bettmann. **56 Library of Congress, Washington, DC:** LC-USZ62-13021. **57 Alamy Stock Photo:** Granger Historical Picture Archive. **58–59 Getty Images:** Ipsumpix / Corbis. **59 Getty Images:** Fotosearch (br). **60 Library of Congress, Washington, DC:** LC-BH826- 3704. **61 Bridgeman Images:** Peter Newark American Pictures. **62 Photoshot:** World History Archive. **63 Getty Images:** Photo12 / UIG. **64–65 Getty Images:** Bettmann. **66 Alamy Stock Photo:** Granger Historical Picture Archive. **67 Getty Images:** Bettmann. **68–69 Getty Images:** Topical Press Agency. **68 Rex by Shutterstock:** Everett Collection (bc). **70 Alamy Stock Photo:** Archive Pics. **71 Getty Images:** US Army Signal Corps / US Army Signal Corps / The LIFE Picture Collection. **72–73 Alamy Stock Photo:** Niday Picture Library. **73 Alamy Stock Photo:** Granger Historical Picture Archive (br). **74–75 Getty Images:** Popperfoto. **74 Getty Images:** Fotosearch (bc). **76–77 Alamy Stock Photo:** Everett Collection Historical. **77 Alamy Stock Photo:** IanDagnall Computing (cr). **78–79 Getty Images:** Bettmann. **80 Getty Images:** New York Times Co. / Hulton Archive. **81 Getty Images:** Bettmann. **82–83 Getty Images:** Bettmann. **82 Alamy Stock Photo:** Everett Collection Historical (bc). **84–85 Getty Images:** Bettmann. **86 Getty Images:** Bettmann. **87 Getty Images:** Ralph Morse / The LIFE Picture Collection. **88–89 Getty Images:** Frank Hurley / NY Daily News Archive. **90 Getty Images:** Rolls Press / Popperfoto. **91 Alamy Stock Photo:** Pictorial Press Ltd. **92–93 Getty Images:** Bettmann. **94 Getty Images:** Hulton Archive. **95 Getty Images:** Archive Holdings Inc.. **96–97 Getty Images:** Arthur Schatz / The LIFE Picture Collection. **98 NASA. 99 Alamy Stock Photo:** Granger Historical Picture Archive. **100–101 Getty Images:** Bettmann. **101 Bridgeman Images:** Pictures from History (br). **102–103 Getty Images:** Diana Walker / Time & Life Pictures. **102 Getty Images:** Karl Schumacher / AFP (bl). **104–105 Getty Images:** Robert R. McElroy. **106 Getty Images:** Dirck Halstead / The LIFE Images Collection. **107 Getty Images:** Bettmann. **108 Alamy Stock Photo:** GL Archive. **109 Getty Images:** Pool Chute Du Mur Berlin / Gamma-Rapho. **110–111 Getty Images:** Cynthia Johnson / Liaison. **111 Alamy Stock Photo:** Richard Ellis. **112–113 Getty Images:** David McNew. **114 Getty Images:** Spencer Platt. **115 Getty Images:** Scott Nelson. **116–117 Alamy Stock Photo:** White House Photo. **119 Getty Images:** Paul J. Richards / AFP. **120 Getty Images:** Anthony Behar-Pool. **120 Alamy Stock Photo:** UrbanImages (bc). **122–123 Alamy Stock Photo:** Ron Adar. **123 Rex by Shutterstock:** Lana Harris / AP (tr) **124–125 Getty Images:** Brooks Kraft LLC / Corbis. **126–127 Getty Images:** Stock Montage. **128 Alamy Stock Photo:** Granger Historical Picture Archive. **129 Alamy Stock Photo:** Granger Historical Picture Archive. **130 Alamy Stock Photo:** Archive Pics. **131 Alamy Stock Photo:** Granger Historical Picture Archive. **132 Getty Images:** Bettmann. **133 Getty Images:** Bettmann. **134–135 Getty Images:** Bettmann. **134 Getty Images:** Bettmann (bc). **136 Getty Images:** Bettmann. **137 Alamy Stock Photo:** CSU Archives / Everett Collection. **138 Rex by Shutterstock:** Everett Collection. **139 Getty Images:** Bettmann.

140 Getty Images: Diana Walker / Time & Life Pictures. **141 akg-images. 142 Getty Images:** Jeffrey Markowitz / Sygma. **143 Getty Images:** Pam Francis / Liaison. **144 Alamy Stock Photo:** White House Photo (bc). **144–145 Photoshot:** Cheriss May. **146–147 Getty Images:** MPI. **148 Getty Images:** Ed Vebell. **49 Alamy Stock Photo:** Niday Picture Library. **150–151 Getty Images:** Bettmann. **152–153 Alamy Stock Photo:** Granger Historical Picture Archive. **153 Getty Images:** Bettmann (tr). **154 Getty Images:** Diana Walker / Time Life Pictures. **155 Getty Images:** Chip Somodevilla. **156–157 Getty Images:** Chip Somodevilla. **157 Getty Images:** Stephen Jaffe / AFP (br). **158–159 Getty Images:** Michael Loccisano. **159 Rex by Shutterstock:** Greg Mathieson (br). **160–161 Getty Images:** MPI. **161 Getty Images:** Universal History Archive (tr). **162–163 akg-images. 162 Alamy Stock Photo:** North Wind Picture Archives (bc). **164–165 Alamy Stock Photo:** Photo Researchers, Inc. **166–167 Getty Images:** Bettmann. **167 akg-images:** Imagno (br). **168–169 Getty Images:** Stock Montage. **169 Alamy Stock Photo:** Archive Pics (br). **169 Library of Congress, Washington, D.C.:** LC-DIG-ds-13272 (br). **170 Getty Images:** Keystone-France / Gamma-Keystone. **171 Getty Images:** Bettmann. **172–173 Alamy Stock Photo:** Holger Hollemann / dpa **174 123RF.com:** Orhan am (cra). **174–175 Dreamstime.com:** Ahdrum. **175 Getty Images:** Bettmann (tr). **176–177 Getty Images:** Eric Draper / The White House. **178 Getty Images:** Bettmann. **179 Getty Images:** Raymond Boyd. **180–181 Dreamstime.com:** Chrisdodutch. **181 Getty Images:** Thomas D. Mcavoy / The LIFE Picture Collection (br). **182 Bridgeman Images:** Everett Collection. **183 Getty Images:** Bettmann. **184 Getty Images:** Smith Collection / Gado (cra); Universal History Archive (tr). **185 123RF.com:** Brenda Kean. **Alamy Stock Photo:** Granger Historical Picture Archive (tr). **186–187 Alamy Stock Photo:** Jesse Kraft. **188 Getty Images:** Sven Creutzmann / Mambo photo; The LIFE Picture Collection (crb). **189 Getty Images:** Alex Wong. **190 Getty Images:** Jewel Samad / AFP. **191 Alamy Stock Photo:** Allstar Picture Library. **192–193 Getty Images:** Raymond Boyd. **196 Alamy Stock Photo:** CSU Archives / Everett Collection (crb/Eugene Debs); The Art Archive (fcl). **Getty Images:** Art Media / Print Collector (tc); Hulton Archive (tr); Encyclopaedia Britannica / UIG (ftr); Kean Collection (cra); Phas / UIG (cl); Hulton Archive (crb); ND / Roger Viollet (cb). **Library of Congress, Washington, DC. 196–197 Dreamstime.com:** Paul Hakimata. **197 US Department of State:** (crb). **White House Historical Association:** (cb). **197 123RF.com:** Visions of America LLC (clb). **Alamy Stock Photo:** GL Archive (cb); GL Archive (cb/Al Gore). **Getty Images:** Bettmann (tl); Bettmann (ftl); Bettmann (tc/Thomas E. Dewey); Bettmann (tr); Bettmann (ftr). **Library of Congress, Washington, DC:** Draper, Eric, 1964 / LC-DIG-ppbd-00371 (crb). **198 123RF.com:** Mikewaters (bc); Visions of America LLC (br). **Getty Images:** Library of Congress / Corbis / VCG (cl). **199 Alamy Stock Photo:** Christopher Victorio / imageSPACE / MediaPunch Inc (br). **201 Alamy Stock Photo:** Luc Novovitch (br).

All other images © Dorling Kindersley

For further information see:
www.dkimages.com